S0-BBR-738

The BOOK *of*
GOOD
HABITS

Simple and Creative Ways
to Enrich Your Life

DIRK MATHISON

Copyright © 1997 by Dirk Mathison

All rights reserved. This book may not be reproduced in whole or in part or in any form or format without written permission of the publisher.

Published by:
SANTA MONICA PRESS
P.O. Box 1076,
Santa Monica, CA 90406-1076
1-800-784-9553

Printed in the United States

This book is intended to provide general information. The publisher, author, distributor, and copyright owner are not engaged in rendering health, medical, legal, financial or other professional advice or services, and are not liable or responsible to any person or group with respect to any loss, illness or injury caused or alleged to be caused by the information found in this book.

Library of Congress Cataloging-in-Publication Data

Mathison, Dirk, 1959—
    The book of good habits : simple and creative ways to enrich your life / by Dirk Mathison.
        p.   cm.
    ISBN 0-9639946-6-2 (pbk.)
    1. Conduct of life.   I. Title.
BJ1581.2.M415   1997
158.1—DC21   97-18710
                                                                                CIP

10 9 8 7 6 5 4 3 2 1

Book and cover design by Lee Fukui

The BOOK of GOOD HABITS

Dear Ann —
for your rich
& very full
life!

SANTA
MONICA
PRESS

Contents

Introduction

What is a habit? It may be as prosaic as flossing, as poetic as taking a moment to consider the setting sun, or as lofty as tackling society's woes. For our purposes, a habit is simply a behavior that repeats throughout the course of daily life.

They are the ways and means of our lives. For better or worse, it's only through the discipline of daily ritual that we achieve our goals. We want good health and an improved physique, but if our routines aren't up to the task, we'll fall short. We need to know more, but if we have poor study habits, the quest is difficult. Virtues like perseverance, kindness and creativity mean little if not put into play.

There's nothing startling about any of this, of course. Chinese scholars, biblical figures and our nation's founding fathers spoke of matters of diet, exercise, and civic involvement long before the arrival of infomercials and self-help books. Jesus spoke to his disciples of the habit of forgiveness. Thomas Jefferson wrote of the importance of afternoon walks and, as was the custom of his day, cleaning one's feet in cold water. Even Mick Jagger speaks of the need to hydrate one's self during lengthy performances.

And habits change along with the era and culture. Most Asians are as off-put by the idea of drinking a cold glass of milk as we are by a bowl of bird's nest soup. Japanese war lords made high ritual of the daily bath. The French aristocracy of Louis XIV did not. In a century, our ancestors will no doubt snicker at stair machines in much the same way we wonder why anyone would attach themselves to one of those vibrating exercise belts.

Clearly, habits, like laws, are made to be broken. Yet many defy both time and country. Most people believe in the benefits of hard work, a disciplined mind, a clean room and vigorous exercise—no matter the path to these ends. And a nice glass of wine with dinner has been a noble addition to the day since the first accidental fermentation of wild grapes.

You, no doubt, will have a hundred other behaviors that we could include here. But I've tried to be universal and practical in my selection. I made them all cheap or free (collecting antiques is a fine habit, but not for everybody). This is a buffet, not a rigid course of instruction, so take what you like and toss the rest.

In searching for past lives, inner children and twelve-step solutions, it seems many of us have forgotten that we should try, first, to just *act* better, even if we're just pretending. This book is based on the simple notion that if we change our daily behavior, our lives will change as well. And that it is through our habits that we give life to our ideas and our ideals.

DIRK MATHISON

I

*A Few Habits
of the Mind...*

1

Be Calm

"He who is calm in mind acquires peacefulness and thus is able to cultivate his mind day and night with more diligence."

BUDDHA

Get out of bed on a daily basis.

Put a single perfect flower in a perfect vase. Consider the curve and color of the flower and the correct vessel for it. Pay attention to its angle of repose. Cut the stem on the bias and to just the right height. Try, in short, to bring the elements into harmony with one another. The Japanese call such flower arrangements "Chabana," and, along with an appreciation for its aesthetics, consider it a relaxing meditation. Such simple acts reduce stress. Chabana is a good starting point for studying the art of "Ikebana," or flower arrangement. Lest some of the men out there think that flowers are for florists, remember that the Samurai practiced Ikebana. And the Samurai were *much* tougher than you will ever be.

"Laziness is nothing more than the habit of resting before you get tired."
JULES RENARD

Do your one thing. Do one thing every day that has nothing to do with work, or being a good parent, or cleaning. Do one thing every day that has no purpose beyond itself, that exists simply for your own selfish and noble pleasure.

Relax your body. Sit quietly and make an effort to calm yourself. Start with the muscles in your face and head and move down to your toes, slowly relaxing all the major muscles while taking deep, slow breaths. Keep your eyes shut and say to yourself, "I am becoming more and more relaxed."

Speak slowly. Rapid speech can lead to a rise in blood pressure and increased heart rate. So speak in a calm, measured tone. Fast talking is not only indicative of stress, but may even induce it.

Breathe while waiting. Take a few deep breaths while waiting in line at the bank or store. Deep-breathing is both relaxing and energizing. And it will take the stress out of a long line and too-few tellers.

"The important thing is to know how to take all things quietly."
FARADAY

Sit up straight. Slouching can restrict breathing and blood flow. So watch your posture when you're tense. Imagine a string going up through the tip of your head, pulling you upright. Keep your shoulder back and head high. When seated, keep your shoulders back, your head high and your feet flat on the ground. Good posture can increase your overall sense of well-being.

Leave home. Spend at least two hours of every day away from home. Even if you work at home. Even if it's snowing. Walk. Go to the mall. Spend time in the company of people rather than appliances and VCRs.

Sing in the shower. You'll breathe more, which means you'll increase your blood flow and thus your energy levels. Stay away from heavy Arias and stick to easy tunes. Avoid "In-A-Gadda-Da-Vida" at all costs.

...Eat shrimp when feeling blue for a dose of mood-elevating selenium ...Take every vacation day ...Wake up slowly ...Travel by train ...Plant trees to commemorate events

Preempt stress. Figure out what raises your blood pressure—rushing to work, shopping when the aisles are packed—and restructure your life to avoid it. For example, shop later in the evening. Wake up ten minutes earlier and forego the morning sports page so that you don't have to rush.

Keep a bottle of champagne in the ice box. Drink it to celebrate the arrival of a letter from a friend, a good nap or a well-made waffle. The flimsiest excuse will do. Likewise with wine—cheap or otherwise.

Take frequent breaks. Every fifteen or twenty minutes, try to look away from the computer or the cash register and drink in a one-minute mental margarita. Studies suggest that productivity improves (especially for dull work) when workers take frequent short breaks. Try day-dreaming for a few seconds, or rolling your shoulders as a way of relieving stress.

And be quick about it. It may seem oxymoronic, but you may have little time to spare for relaxation. So learn to relax quickly. Give yourself triggers: As you put the key in the door of your house, for example, turn off stress and begin to relax. Try counting backward from twenty to zero and imagine yourself walking down a grassy hill towards relaxation.

Keep it below sixty. Try not to work more than sixty hours a week, including drive time. Any more than this and you may start to burn out. A long work week does more to increase the stress level of Americans than any other single factor. So see what you can do to work less. For example, ask for an extra week or two of vacation in place of a raise. Perhaps you can convince your boss to experiment with the four-day work week. Many companies (especially in Germany, where

. . . Use candles even when there's no special occasion . . . Keep your shoes shined because it's hard to feel bad with shiny shoes . . . And favor any drink that contains an umbrella . . .

such a schedule has become popular), find that working a ten-hour day for four days in exchange for an extra day of rest has done wonders to help workers relax and be more productive. Some employees (especially moms) have tried job-sharing, in which you and a partner split the work-week in half.

And keep it below ten. If your "To Do" list adds up to more than ten hours, try to edit it down to a more reasonable number of tasks.

Give yourself twenty... When scheduling for a hectic day, give yourself a buffer of twenty per-cent more time. It's important to realize that life usually takes longer than expected. So estimate how long a given task will take and add a fifth.

Move on from regret...
"The one who follows the noble path to enlightenment will not maintain regrets, neither will he cherish anticipations, but with an equitable and peaceful mind, will meet what comes."

Welcome change...
"The wise man learns to meet the changing circumstance of life with an equitable spirit, being neither elated by success nor depressed by failure."

Carpe diem...
*"The secret of health for both mind and
body is not to mourn for the past, not to worry about the
future, or not to anticipate troubles,
but to live wisely and earnestly for the present."*

And control yourself...
*"To enjoy good health, to bring true happiness
to one's family, to bring peace to all, one must first
discipline and control one's own mind."*
CHINESE PROVERBS

*Organize...
If you're tense,
reorganizing a
closet or a garage
can help you chill
out by giving you
a sense of control
over the chaos
of the universe.*

Be in attendance at the Laughing Club. A gentleman in India observed—correctly—that laughing does wonders to reduce stress levels. He began a small club devoted solely to laughing. Members gather and spend an hour or two guffawing their way to lower blood pressure and a bolstered immune system. There are now Laughing Clubs in every corner of India. If you can't get to the humid sub-continent, start your own laughing club with a friend or two. Try a Marx brothers movie, or that "Lucy" episode with the candies on the conveyor belt. Make it a habit to laugh your way towards relaxation.

Be quiet... Spend twenty minutes of each day in silence. Call it meditation, prayer or whatever you like, but a few minutes spent in contemplative quiet can help you become more content. It's a time, perhaps, to tell yourself what you want. Or to think of nothing at all. Just breathe, from both the stomach and the chest. Meditation lowers blood pressure and breathing rate, along with the blood level of lactate, a chemical associated with muscle tension. A few moments of meditation make the body less vulnerable to such stress hormones as adrenaline.

Observe the Sabbath... Even if you're as atheistic as Mao, try to set aside one day a week for relaxation and contemplation. You may not want to be as stringent as many Orthodox Jews, who won't drive cars or turn on lights between the sunsets of Friday and Saturday, but you may find that a day without chores can become an enriching habit.

...Do fifteen or twenty push-ups to get those endorphins flowing for an immediate fix ...Avoid the phone before breakfast ...Make big decisions and get haircuts only when you're calm ...Avoid self-pity as if it were e-coli

Balance memories...When you remember a painful incident from your past, balance it with a happy memory from the same period. Psychologists believe that a great deal of our stress comes from painful memories working their way back into consciousness. So try to remember the good times along with the bad and you may feel better.

And sedate yo'self...If breathing and flowers don't quite cut it, try some mild tranquilizers. Drink a cup of either valerian or chamomile tea before bed. Both of these herbs are age-old sedatives. Or have some L-tryptophan in the form of a glass of warm milk.

Cry...Your body has developed a wonderful way of relieving stress. It's called crying. So don't hold back. A good cry is very relaxing. Remember what Charles Dickens wrote in *Oliver Twist*: "It opens the lungs, washes the countenance, exercises the eyes, and softens down the temper. So cry away." Rock...Invest in a good rocking chair and use it to relax while watching television. It

...Crush the needles of an incense cedar into your hand, then breathe deeply ...Drink cold beer while eating hot popcorn...Go dancing at least once a month...

provides a small measure of exercise, increases blood flow and helps stretch. And make love...Sex helps relieve tension headaches and muscle aches. It is very relaxing. Like you need an excuse.

...Keep a pair of tennis shoes at the office so you can take a quick run or power walk during breaks ...Rub your temples and the back of your neck with your fingertips

Challenge yourself for relaxation. There's so little leisure time these days that you should make an effort to take full advantage of off-hours. Psychologists say that the best way to feel truly refreshed and renewed is not to zone out on the couch. Instead, try activities that require concentration, like rock-climbing or bicycling. You don't have to climb Everest, but your hobbies should be a constant source of challenge. These challenges should be completely different from those you face at work or home. Do not, for example, build a new shed in the backyard for relaxation if you're in construction.

Imagine the solution. When relaxed, visualize yourself coming to grips and solving a vexing problem. If a solution can be imagined, it can usually be accomplished. If you face a struggle ahead, whether it's emotional or financial, think of your problem as a challenge to be overcome. It may not turn your woes into a kind of sport, but it may help you keep your wits and humor about you.

Accept change with optimism. Change is life. It does not mean that the world is crumbling. Consider the 103-year-old Okinawan woman who, when asked her secret to longevity, answered that it is, simply, to "Welcome Change." So accept life's changes with optimism rather than anxiety.

Clean your desk at the end of the day...Get rid of anything you don't need. Put long-term projects in a folder and set it aside. It helps give a sense of closure to the work day, which means your night will be more relaxing. It also helps you start fresh the next day. And it saves time, since you won't need to search through piles of useless papers. You can also try making a "To Do" list at the end of the day, which is a small psychological trick to help you literally leave your worries on your desk instead of bringing them home.

...Wiggle a bit every fifteen minutes or so to help avoid stiffness and muscle stress ...Keep an old pair of boots in your trunk and if you see a safe, inviting wooded path off the side of the road, stop for a quick walk...

Pet dogs...Even if you don't own an animal, studies indicate that petting a poodle (or a Great Dane—the choice is yours) can lower blood pressure and stress indicators. Many rest homes and convalescent hospitals have noted the recuperative power of dogs. So seek out a dog and, if it's not a snarling, vicious beast, pet him for the sake of your heart.

And linger in the beautiful foolishness of things...

"The afternoon is glowing, brightening the bamboo, the fountains are bubbling with delight, the soughing of the pines is heard in our kettle. Let us dream of evanescence, and linger in the beautiful foolishness of things."
OSAKURA KAKUZO in *The Book of Tea*

2

Vacate

*"Lay out all your clothes and all your money.
Then, take half the clothes and twice the money."*
SUSAN BUTLER ANDERSON

Clear off your desk... The best way to relax on an expensive get-away is to tidy up all unfinished business before heading off to paradise. It allows you to make your return to the world that much easier. Cut the lines of communication. Do not check in for messages. Do not call your secretary or boss. Do not check your e-mail. The point of a vacation is to vacate. Those commercials showing men and women happily working away at their computers as they lounge on a tropical beach are not a promise of a utopia to come, but a nightmarish Orwellian threat to all that is good in the world. Be *way* out of touch. Pretend your office and its various tortures do not exist. You'll have a much nicer time.

Travel when the leaves begin to fall... In autumn, the screaming teenagers of summer are back in school, and the hordes have returned to work. The weather is still good. Many spots offer discounts (including cruises at twenty-five percent off) to attract business during the off-season. So take your vacation in September or October.

And bring wine. When flying a long distance, bring along a bottle of good wine, a corkscrew and two cups. Share it with your seat mate (whether you know him or not), if he or she desires, and you'll have a much nicer flight. This, of course, goes against the conventional wisdom that one should not drink on planes because it is, God forbid, *dehydrating*. Travelers are advised to drink water like camels because of the desert air

...Take a fold-up bag to carry home all those antiquities ...Pick up airline tickets at the travel agent to save time ...Wear earplugs to avoid airplane din ...Open your suitcase as soon as you arrive at your destination and if anything's missing, call the authorities immediately...

on Boeings. So drink water along with the wine and make a new friend.

Pay for airline tickets with a credit card...You usually get automatic life insurance, and if you pay in cash or by check, you could be denied curb-side check-in. In this age of heightened concern over terrorism, airlines want to be able to trace their passengers before their luggage gets on the plane. Paying with a credit card makes them feel comfortable.

Pack for triple duty...Bring clothing that you can wear in a variety of situations. Bring pants, for example, that are casual but can be dressed up with a coat for more formal affairs. Always bring a pair of shorts that you can use for both running and swimming. Many hotels have indoor pools, so you may be able to take a few laps even in the dead of winter. Remember, too, to pack the heavy stuff on the bottom of your suitcase to prevent crushing. Put toiletries in a waterproof container, and your shoes in a bag to keep them from soiling your clothes. Hang everything up as soon as you arrive.

...Pack a disposable panorama camera ...Take incense to freshen up hotel rooms...Ask for exit-row seats for more leg room ...Hang your clothes in the bathroom while you shower to get rid of wrinkles...

And then bring it on the plane. Have everything you need in your carry-on bag. It's safe to assume that at some point, your luggage will be shipped to Oakland while you're en route to Auckland. So keep money, toiletries and a change of clothes with you in your carry-on luggage. Keep any credit cards you won't be using at home in case your wallet is stolen or lost while traveling. Consider shipping extra luggage. Your luggage is less likely to get lost through Fed Ex or UPS then at an airline baggage terminal. It will make travel easier, and may also help prevent muscle strain or sore backs from lifting heavy bags.

Leave early... Try to leave on the first flights of the day. The earlier you leave, the less likely it will be that your plane is delayed by the ripple-effect of late flights. And check your airfare after you've bought your ticket. If the fare has gone down (which happens all the time), the airline will usually refund the difference, but only if you ask.

And ask for more. There's little harm in making a polite request for an upgrade to business class, especially if you're a frequent flyer member. Do the same at hotels. Tell them you're a regular and ask for an executive suite instead of a regular room. Pick a time when they're not busy, or when the hotel doesn't seem over-booked. Don't try it if the person behind the counter seems tense and overworked.

Use the stars as your blanket. Bring along a sleeping bag, and sleep outdoors as often as you can. Check with travel guides and local tourist information centers to find out the best (and safest) campgrounds. Many campgrounds have amenities like showers and pools at a fraction of the cost of hotels. And you get to sleep outside, which is one of the better ways to shake off the dust of civilization.

Walk the plane. On long flights, get out of your seat at least every thirty minutes to stretch and exercise. Studies indicate that a little workout on the plane lessens the impact of jet lag and prevents muscle and neck stiffness. It also makes the flight go faster.

Give yourself some room...Even on a family vacation (or especially on a family vacation), you should allow yourself some time alone or with a spouse, even if it's just for an hour or two for a stroll along the beach. But go with the flow. If the group decides that they're in the mood to see the shrunken head exhibit, either bow out gracefully or go see the heads. Compromise is critical during family vacations, so don't be dictatorial. If you have kids, let them help plan the agenda to some extent.

And take a vacation from your vacation. Schedule a few days of rest in your travel plans so that you can recharge your batteries. Use the time to think about what you've seen. Let yourself soak it all in.

Come back a day early. Returning for a day of rest and recuperation helps soothe that return-to-work shock we've all experienced. So try to rest before heading back to the office.

3

Be a Scholar

*"Every man who knows how to read has it
in his power to magnify himself,
to multiply the ways in which he exists,
to make his life full, significant and interesting."*
ALDOUS HUXLEY

Question... Learning is not passive. It takes an active mind to absorb new material. So when you're reading, either in leisure or in a classroom setting, ingrain a few good habits. If there are concepts in the material that aren't clear to you, write them down in the form of a question. For example, "Why is a wide band width important for digital information?" Sometimes, simply asking the right question can help you understand the material. At the very least, it will lead you in the right direction.

Tell a friend... When studying, get a loved one to indulge you for a few moments. Tell them what you've learned and what you think of what you've learned. Give special attention to areas that are still unclear to you. Get your friends to ask questions. Sometimes the best way to learn is to talk it out. Then teach. Tutor a friend or classmate in material you yourself are trying to absorb. It will force you to have a clear understanding of the information.

And keep your mouth shut. Reading aloud or moving one's lips is not only an annoyance to the person next to you at the library, it also inhibits both comprehension and reading speed. The same is true of using one's finger to follow the words as you read, or using a ruler, which makes for less-effective learning. So read silently, without moving your lips.

Avoid excuses...

"Do not say you will study when you have leisure; perhaps you will never have leisure."
HILLEL
a Rabbi and scholar
of ancient Israel

Study before bed. Research indicates that people who cram just before nodding off seem to retain more information than those who study earlier. So go over notes for a test or a presentation just before going to sleep. And relax. It's not worth losing sleep over.

Read at the library. Find a quiet corner, turn off the cell phone, and spend a few hours every month reading in the company of great books.

Read during commercials. Read short items while the ad for beer is on T.V. It's better than not reading at all.

Read yourself to sleep. For many of us, the only time for a good book is in that precious half-hour or so before sleep. Why waste the moment with a re-run when you could be polishing off a few pages of Walt Whitman?

Look it up. We all encounter verbiage that we may find obtuse and nebulous. Keep a dictionary handy to abrogate obfuscation. The penultimate

"I'm not very good at it myself, but the first rule about spelling is that there is only one z in 'iz'."

ABRAHAM LINCOLN

rubric for accrual of phraseology is the mobilization of a dictionary.

Find the perfect word. There's usually a better, simpler word waiting out there. Keep a thesaurus by your side even when writing small notes or business letters. You're not going to impress anyone with words like "abrogate" when "eliminate" does just as well. A thesaurus can help you be clear and concise.

Have reel good gramer. Use "both" commas, and, quotations, sparingly. Don't be a guy who, like, uses no double negatives and random colloquialisms. Remember that clichés are a dime a dozen, and that big words are often unnecessary and superfluous. Don't mix your metaphors like some turgid green thumb. Don't be repetitive, or repeat yourself. And it goes without saying that it goes without saying. And remember to avoid exclamation points at all costs! They are appropriate for junior high love notes and novels with bare-chested men on the cover, but little else. So shun them! And have a nice day!

Identify the Big Stuff. Highlight key words and phrases that will help you recall the main themes of your material. For example, if you're learning to sail and are reading about the various points of sail, you'd underline "Beam Reach," "Close Haul" and "In Irons," to name a few.

Screen. During lectures (which, by the way, are not just for college students) learn to listen actively for key words and phrases. Screen out the rest of the jetsam and flotsam and remember the major points. Your mind is an amazing tool, but it is not a storage shed.

Forget remembering. Consider the material as a whole. It is better for you to comprehend the intent of a writer or professor than for you to remember individual words or facts. It often happens that if you have a real grasp of the core intent of the material, it follows that you will recall its details.

Rewrite it. Write down the key points of material you've just read, even if they're already in print. It will help you clarify and distill the material. And support the index card industry. Write down one crystalline, distilled idea per card when studying. Use them later as grown-up versions of flash cards.

Minimalize. When taking notes, try to boil down concepts to a few key words. Verbatim dictation does little but overload you with information. You can always consult secondary sources later.

Elmnt Vwls. Whn tkng nts, frgt vwls. Or just wrt the beg of wrds like rep or vid. Nts wll be fstr & easr to tk.

Dog Ear. Unless you're dealing with some rare first-edition, bend back the corner of pages that are most significant. Or use paper clips.

> *"I have given up reading books;*
> *I find it takes my mind off myself."*
> OSCAR LEVANT

4

Remember to Remember

"I might repeat to myself, slowly and soothingly,
a list of quotations beautiful from minds profound—
if I can remember any of the damn things."
DOROTHY PARKER

Remember to remember. Five minutes after absorbing new information, go over the key elements of the material in your head. Don't worry if you've forgotten some of it. Do the same thing after another hour or two, then again. It is a way of packing the new data into long-term storage.

Ask questions. If you must remember, say, the specific gravity of chocolate milk, be like a "Jeopardy" contestant and put it into your head in the form of a question. Or, when putting down an umbrella, ask yourself, "Where am I putting the umbrella? By the front door." It is an effective way of storing information amidst the neural pathways.

Pay attention. An inability to remember a name or fact is often a simple matter of laziness. So when you're learning a new fact or name, perk up. Make it an active process rather than a passive one. Don't assume that you will remember, but understand that it will take a bit of effort on your part. Memory is not, like a beating heart, an automatic response.

Have habits. It's a good habit to be habituated. Leave your keys, wallets, stamps, purse, etc. in the same spot every night and you will likely remember where they are. Study in the same place to ingrain it as ritual. Use your kitchen timer as a reminder to pick up the kids. Or to call the gas company, or to leave for an appointment. It has more uses than for cooking eggs.

Play Games. One of the best and easiest ways to keep your mental acuity intact is with a game of chess. Or a challenging crossword puzzle. Or a game of bridge.

Associate... Link a person or a thing to a prominent characteristic. Robert can become "Robert Red Hair" or Machiavelli can become "Conniving Machiavelli." Barney can become "Big Purple Barn."

Elaborate... When trying to commit a fact or name to memory, place it in a memorable context. For example, the name "Mark" can become "Dark Mark," or the word "insouciance" ("carefree") can be committed to memory using the sentence, "She was carefree enough to be in a soup seance."

And alphabetize... If you're attempting to remember all that you must do in a day, or studying a rote list of minerals for class, try alphabetizing the collection. It's not just a way of remembering a specific list; it's also a good way to develop one's memory in the same way one works a bicep at the gym.

...Exercise, because studies indicate that older folks who exercise as much as younger folks retain similar levels of neurological function...Eat baked potatoes, because they're loaded with vitamin B6, which may help boost your long-term memory...

Give it a place...Try to link a fact with a common household item. The item and fact need not bear any resemblance to each other or have anything in common. If, for example, you're trying to remember the date of Columbus' arrival in America, link in your mind the year 1492 to, say, the piano bench. When you search your memory for the date (or name, or formula), you will have cross-indexed the information. Again, there's no relation between the two items except for the fact that you've bound them together in your mind in order to jump-start your memory.

Tell yourself a story... Try to make up a story that uses the information you're trying to remember. Example—a license plate that reads "WBF 765" can be recalled as "A white buffalo fell 765 times."

And write it down before you forget. Because you *will* forget. You'll be at Safeway and forget the chopped walnuts. Or at your office and forget the brilliant idea about cutting production costs. So write it down.

Memorize a few stanzas...

> *"Since my childhood I have had a strong taste*
> *for poetry, and I willingly learned by heart long*
> *passages from our great poets."*
> MADAM MARIE CURIE

Notice details. Try to remember your professor's lapel pin, or the way the light came into the room while you were reading. It is a way of installing "triggers" that will help you recall the bulk of the information.

Do memory push-ups...Think of your memory as a muscle that needs a good amount of exercise. At some point every day, try to remember a half-dozen obscure facts: your phone number from childhood, your high school locker combination, the name of your ex-husband. It's as simple as a Kiegel exercise and an effective way of dusting off your brain's cobwebs. Or just remember the room. Memorize ten items while waiting in line at the grocery store. Or a few dates off magazines in the doctor's office. Try to recall them after you've left.

Be repetitive. Repeat the fact at every opportunity, either in conversation or to one's self. If you've just met someone, try introducing them around the room. Or say something like, "Well, Jake, how long have you been at the party? Do you know the host, Jake?" They may think you're a bit thick, but you'll remember their name.

And be repetitive.

5

Throw Spears

"Don't play the saxophone. Let it play you."
CHARLIE PARKER

Be like director Ingmar Bergman, who has the habit of using this specific bit of visualization to help with the creative process: "If you can imagine," he says, "I throw a spear into the dark. That is my intuition, and then I have to send an expedition into the jungle to find the spear and to find a way to the spear. And that is absolutely another process. That is my intellect." This is Bergman's method. Try to find your own habits for giving your creative self a bit of a push.

Play against type. Make it a habit to do something totally out of character once a month or so. Spend a Sunday afternoon painting watercolors instead of watching football. Go see a professional wrestling match instead of the symphony.

Seek out unknown titles. Read books that no one else reads. You'll have access to thoughts that few possess and achieve a measure of independence that you would not otherwise reach. You'll be original. Forget Stephen King for a while. Try *The Book of Tea*, *Dreams from Bunker Hill*, or *Bats Fly at Dusk*.

Look at old art. Many of us wait until we're in a foreign country before we step foot in a museum, even though a stroll among great art can be an inspiring habit. Take advantage of museums in your area. Keep abreast of upcoming exhibits by reading the Sunday arts section. A good art show is one of the major benefits of living in a metropolitan area. If your time is limited, ask the docent what she would recommend seeing first at the museum.

And look for inspiration wherever you think you might find it...

"I get the ideas going. Then I write down, I copy out of any books that stimulate me at the time, many quotations, and I keep it. And I put down the source. Then when it comes to the actual work, I keep a complete record of the steps. I keep note of every dance I have."
MARTHA GRAHAM

Be like DaVinci. Leonardo DaVinci is renowned not only for his great genius, but because he had the foresight to leave such a rich legacy of that genius. He had the habit of sketching his ideas (a helicopter and submarine, for example) in a sketch pad, much as a writer uses a journal. DaVinci understood full well that, as he says, a few lines capture "knowledge which is impossible for ancient or modern writers to convene without an infinitely tedious example and confused pro-lixity of writing and time." So be like Leo and keep a pad on hand to make a visual note of ideas—a new way to organize a closet, replant-ing a garden, or a new wing of the house. Don't be fancy. Just get the idea down fast for the sake of memory and inspiration. You may not have DaVinci's genius, but you can adopt his methods.

... Write Haiku on Easter eggs with styptic pencils, and then eat the eggs before they start to smell like sulfur ... Stop at weird roadside museums ... Listen to music in the bath

Question art. When you look at a new piece of art, ask yourself a few questions: How do you feel when you look at it? Why do you feel the way you do? If you like it, why? If not, why not? What is the artist trying to say? What is the artist's perspective on the material? Is it an emotional message, or is the artist trying to say something specific about the human condition? What is it *not*? Or sit down with a pad and try to do a sketch of a painting. It's a wonderful way of appreciating and understanding the art, even if you can't draw to save your life.

Paint after sunup... Try getting up just before sunup and working on a watercolor over your morning coffee. Try painting from memory. It's fine to paint a scene as it unfolds before your eyes, but many artists prefer to work from memory. Thus, they become not just cameras, but interpreters. The art then possesses something of their soul. It rises above mediocrity. If you choose to paint from a natural scene, try using an empty photo slide to help you get a sense of the painting's composition.

Or just trace...Even if you have no inherent ability as an artist, you can still trace over other people's work. Use tracing paper to outline, say, architectural drawings of the Pantheon in Rome. Or the detail on a Ming vase. Tracing offers a better understanding—and bond—with the original work. It may give you a few new ideas.

But be original.

> *"Most people are other people.*
> *Their thoughts are someone else's opinions,*
> *their lives a mimicry,*
> *their passions a quotation."*
> OSCAR WILDE

Keep an "ideas" folder...Throw in those cocktail napkins with your brilliant ideas for screenplays and better mousetraps. Or your DaVinci-like

...Buy art for love, not money...Photograph flowers during early blooms and in a setting that suggests a strong composition ...Go to free poetry readings...

sketches. You may read the idea the next day and swear off martinis, or you may decide to build that mousetrap.

And a journal. It is one of life's best habits. Even if it's just a line or two a day, it offers a measure of semblance to a chaotic world. Even for non-writers, a journal entry helps give a bit of badly-needed perspective to the events of the day. You may find that looking back at a journal entry may help with relationships or business dealings. Those stray ideas we all have—some brilliant, some not-so-brilliant—will have found a permanent home on paper.

Freeze up a mess of peaches and cream. During writer Jack Kerouac's travels back and forth across the country, he once stayed at a farmhouse where the young couple did their best to entertain their guest. They offered Kerouac a bowl of peaches that they stuck in the freezer with cream, and apologized for their lack of big-city, store-bought ice cream. Kerouac said it was probably the only real ice cream he'd ever eaten.

So eat frozen peaches and cream and think about simple pleasures.

Know how things work…Can you explain— really explain—how a telephone works? A television? A computer printer? How information is stored on a floppy disc? Make it a habit to have at least a general understanding of how the technology that surrounds us operates. It may help generate an idea or two of your own. Consult books like *The Way Things Work* by David Macauly, or *Popular Mechanics*. This is especially helpful if you're the parent of a bright eight-year-old, who will undoubtedly know much more about the natural world then you ever did.

And explore new avenues…

> *"Don't expect me to repeat myself.*
> *My past does not interest me any more.*
> *Rather than recopy myself,*
> *I would prefer to recopy others."*
> PABLO PICASSO

II

On Matters of
Health and Safety
in a Terribly
Treacherous World

6

Comb Your Hair

"Hair and teeth—a man got those
two things, he's got it all."
JAMES BROWN

Keep thy urine clear. We all know to drink eight glasses of water a day. It's one of the best habits you can have. A simple way to tell if you're hydrated is by the color of your urine. If it's clear, it means you're doing just fine. If it's a darker yellow, drink more fluids until it becomes less opaque. If your urine's clear, it means your skin is probably getting all the moisture it needs—one of the single most important factors in determining its health.

Use while wet. Use moisturizer when your skin is still damp from the shower. Moisturizers are concocted to trap moisture, so if your skin is still moist, all the better. The more moisture in your skin, the less evident those wrinkles will be.

"Water is good. It benefits all things."
LAO TSE

Moisturize your lips. Licking your lips only dries them out. Try a dab of petroleum jelly, especially in the winter, to keep lips from chapping. Rub petroleum jelly on your hands after doing dishes to prevent dryness. And chill the air. Put a big bowl of ice in front of a table fan. It will both cool and moisturize the air, and keep your skin in better condition.

Go out in the noonday sun. If you are troubled by your youthful appearance and wish, for the sake of your standing in the community, to look old as soon as possible, get out there and bake. Forget sunscreen. Try, instead, to use baby oil for that deep-down burn. You should, by your mid-thirties, have the distinguished look of a person in their mid-fifties.

Eat garlic… The ancient priests of Egypt considered this cousin to the onion to be an abomination among vegetables. We know better. Studies indicate that garlic may increase the life of the billions of cells that make up your skin. It may inhibit the growth of cancer cells, boost the immune system and provide a natural antibacterial component. Just look at the condemned criminals of the 16th century who, forced to bury those done in by the Plague, staved off the disease with a potent mix of raw garlic and red wine. If you're concerned about bad breath, try deodorized garlic pills. Otherwise eat it raw or in sauces.

Use cheap wash cloths… The cheaper the washcloth, the more likely it is to be rough. So cheaper washcloths make for better ex-foliants, which means they're better at taking the dead, rotting skin off your face.

And blot your face dry. Don't wipe water off your face with a towel. Over time, this harsh

"I can't take a well-tanned person seriously."
CLEVELAND AMORY

treatment can exacerbate wrinkles and cause a few new ones. Better to gently blot at the skin, using the towel like a sponge instead of a rag.

Brush for a song. The average tooth brushing takes about forty-five seconds. Dentists say that to effectively remove plaque, you should go at it for about two minutes. Try brushing to the radio for the duration of one song. And don't forget the tongue. You can brush your teeth for the duration of a symphony and not alleviate bad breath. Most foul breath begins with a collection of bacteria on the tongue. It lingers there, feeding off dead tissue and giving off malodorous, sulfuric fumes (make it a habit to forget this while enjoying a kiss). So brush not just your teeth, but your entire tongue, gums, and the roof of your mouth.

Floss with foam. Forget the debate about whether to brush before or after flossing. Do it while there's still some toothpaste in your mouth. The foam will help the floss glide in between your teeth.

…Eat parsley to keep your breath clean…Steam your face over a hot sink full of water to clean pores

Use wooden hangers. Joan Crawford was *right*. Wire hangers are bad for clothes. They leave those lines that can weaken fabric and shorten the life of the garment. So stick with wooden or plastic hangers.

Get a haircut, kid. Even if you like long hair, don't go for more than three months without a trim. If you wait too long, you'll get split ends. Don't get your hair cut when you're under emotional duress. You may feel like you need a "change" and ask for some stupid look that you'll regret.

Massage the scalp... Brush your hair a bit before shampooing to loosen the dirt. Then rub your scalp vigorously while shampooing. It improves circulation, is relaxing, and helps insure that you're getting rid of all the nasty bits that have accumulated. Use your fingertips and rub your scalp as if you were kneading bread. Likewise, when kneading bread, act as if you were rubbing your scalp.

... Cut toenails straight across rather than rounding them... Add fresh herbs to bath water to smell like a romp in the woods...

And then air-dry it. Avoid the use of blow-dryers that can damage your hair by drying it out. Instead, when possible, let your hair dry in the air. Rub your fingers through it as it dries. If you're in a hurry, go ahead and blow it dry, but leave it slightly damp.

Be conservative with scents. Remember that your odor, store-bought or otherwise, should not enter the room before you do. Heed the advice of Estée Lauder, who said, "The best way to apply fragrance is to spray it into the air and walk into it."

7

Eat Your Vegetables

> *"Health food makes me sick."*
> CALVIN TRILLIN

Drink green tea from a blue cup. The ancient Chinese poet Luwhoh believed green tea should be served in a brilliant blue ceramic cup to enhance its color and thus its flavor. Tea is, to many cultures, much more than mere beverage. It is also a means by which one can discover the very great in the very small details of life. Green teas, as it happens, also contain polyphenols— compounds that reduce the free radicals that cause serious cell damage. Which simply rein-

49

forces the Zen teaists' belief that if we just look, we'll find perfection in the commonplace.

Be like the Vileambabbaians. The people of Vileambabba, Ecuador have one of the longest life-spans on earth. They live under the auspices of a few simple habits that you may want to embrace: One, walk over a mile a day. Two, shun processed foods. Three, eat meat sparingly. And four, don't worry so much about your kids (this alone should add a few years).

Be lean and complex. Eat a mixture of lean protein and complex carbs at each meal, including breakfast. Although carbohydrates are the body's main source of energy, too many can cause something called "reactive hypoglycemia," which can leave you feeling drained. Complex carbs like whole wheat bread or brown rice digest slowly, releasing sugars into the system at an even pace. Mixing this with a lean protein means that you won't be overdoing the carbs, which in turn results in a stable blood sugar level and increased energy. So start the day with a mix of carbs and protein (skim milk with whole-grain cereal, or egg whites with wheat bread, for example) for a burst of energy. Try to eat as soon as possible after waking to get the day off to a good start. Have the first cup of coffee with breakfast instead of before you eat to keep your appetite healthy. Or...

Skip breakfast. If you long for a day of lethargy, bad breath, lack of focus and exhaustion, just go without the first meal of the day. It's not that important.

Eat like a horse. That is to say, eat oatmeal. It's one of nature's best sources of slow-burning complex carbohydrates. Studies indicate that oatmeal increases athletic endurance, perhaps because of its high level of soluble fiber, which in turn slows the release of carbohydrates into the system. You should also make it a habit to eat unusual grains. Try kasha and amaranth. The carbohydrates in grains are the building blocks of energy. They contain vital nutrients and fibers. So make it a habit to experiment with grains you've never eaten before, like quinoa from South America.

Eat early and often. Eat five or six meals instead of three big ones. One of the keys to energy and weight loss is the maintenance of a stable blood sugar level. If you eat small meals more often, your blood sugar will remain constant throughout the day. You'll avoid the kind of ravenous hunger that leads us crawling to a Big Mac. Try eating a high-fiber snack in the afternoon. A three-o'clock snack of cereal and non-fat milk will give you a boost during a slouchy time of day. It will also increase your intake of fiber, which has a number of vital health benefits. And it will make you less ravenous for dinner, which means you'll make better nutritional choices at the end of the day.

Keep a big fruit salad in the refrigerator. Make a huge fruit salad, add a little lemon juice, and keep it in the fridge as a side dish or healthy snack. If it's already made, you're more likely to reach for

...Drink calcium-fortified orange juice...Shop when you're full... Aerobicize to raise your body's level of good cholesterol ...Moisten sandwiches with veggies like tomatoes instead of using mayo

it instead of the Ho-Hos. Americans should eat two to three servings of fruit per day, so try to have a bowl with every meal.

Use phylo dough. It's much lower in fat than pie dough, and can be kept in the freezer for months. You can buy it ready-made at most grocery stores. Try several different brands until you find one you like. Try sprinkling apples, sugar and cinnamon into some phylo dough, then baking until crusty brown for a low-fat and fast apple pie. Wrap it around a turkey meat loaf for a poorman's Wellington.

...Dip bacon in cold water to keep it from curling up ...Eat Chinese food in bed straight from the carton while watching a video...

Seek out lower-fat versions of foods you like. Use non-fat sour cream instead of cream in casseroles. Or chicken broth instead of butter. Experiment a bit and you'll probably find that you can do without fats without sacrificing too much flavor.

Sprinkle. Sprinkle wheat germ on baked potatoes for increased fiber. Or almonds in your salad for cholesterol-reducing calcium and vitamins.

Eat the pulp. Don't forget to eat the white pulp in citrus fruits. They contain flavonoids, a potent anti-cancer compound.

Or chunks of apples for fiber and sweetness. Or lecithin, which may improve both mood and memory. Or baked oatmeal into soups or salads. Sprinkle in a handful of parsley to sauces or pastas to up your intake of beta-carotene and vitamin C and fiber. Sprinkling is an easy way to improve nutrition and add taste to food.

And eat raisins. Studies indicate that "resveratol," a compound found in the dried fruit, may lower blood levels of low density lipids or LDLs (the bad cholesterol). Resveratol is also in wine, which may explain why the French, who eat all those rich foods, have remarkably low blood cholesterol levels.

Perform the first nose on white linen. The best time to taste wine is at about ten in the morning when your palate has yet to be corrupted by the day's taint. It's best to display the wine on white linen to bring out its color. When smelling the wine for the first time (the "first nose," as it's called), stick your proboscis well into the glass and exhale from your lungs before breathing in.

When tasting, remember to exploit all your taste buds—from the tip of your tongue all the way to the back of your mouth.

Eat power lunches. Eat a combination of lean protein and whole grains (example—turkey on whole wheat bread, hold the mayo, and a glass of non-fat milk) and fruit. Don't get weighed down by a burger and fries. You'll have more energy to get you through the afternoon, and you'll keep the weight off. Some research indicates that you should eat the protein first so that the carbs, which can make you drowsy, reach the brain later. This sounds rather difficult, especially when eating a sandwich, but try it to see if it makes a difference.

Keep the good stuff on display. Keep fruit and vegetables that don't need refrigeration in a bowl on the center of the table. Don't hide it in the back of the fridge, where you may discover it weeks later as a green puddle. You're more likely to eat something if you know it's in the household.

Chill. Store your coffee beans in the fridge to keep them fresh, not in the freezer where they will lose some of their oil content, and thus flavor.

Seek out the unchopped...Frozen fruits and vegetables are better left uncut. Chopping increases the amount of surface area, which in turn leads to a loss of vitamins and nutrients. So buy whole spears of frozen broccoli or whole leaf spinach instead of the chopped variety. Frozen foods that have been properly handled may contain even more vitamins than fresh, since they're often processed right out of the fields.

Think of kidneys and cannelini...Beans reduce blood cholesterol. A simple, fast way to up your intake is to add a can of beans to your vegetable soup. It not only makes your soup heartier without adding many calories, but it also reduces the LDLs in your system. And it tastes good. Try running the canned beans in water to help rinse away some of the simple sugars that we can't digest. You'll have less gas (having less gas is a good habit).

And save the whey. You know that liquid that separates out of cottage cheese and yogurt? It contains whey (as in "curds and whey") and some sports physicians believe it to be one of the world's best sources of protein. It's also full of B vitamins and calcium. So stir it back into the cottage cheese instead of draining it off.

Go easy on condiments...

> "Americans can eat garbage, provided you sprinkle it liberally with ketchup, mustard, chili sauce, Tabasco sauce, cayenne pepper, or any other condiment which destroys the original flavor of the dish."
> HENRY MILLER

Eat fewer calories as the day progresses. When day turns to night, your metabolism begins to slow, which means fewer and fewer calories burnt. Yet most of us eat our biggest meal when our bodies are least able to use the energy it provides. So make it a habit to eat more calorically-dense food during the day when you need it the most. If you eat too many calories in the evening, there's a good chance they'll store as body fat.

Forget the last inch of Kung-Pao. Leave the last bit of Chinese food in its container. This is where much of the sauce (and thus fat) will settle. This can spare you from dozens of grams of fat with little or no loss in flavor. Keep canned soup in the refrigerator. The cold will cause the fat to congeal at the top of the can. Use a spoon to scrape it off before preparing. Or throw an ice cube into warm soup. A lot of the fat will cling to it.

Blot...Use paper towels to blot the grease off pizza, hamburgers, fried chicken—whatever your poison may be. You'll save yourself several hundred calories and lose not one whit of taste.

Ignore instructions...Reduce the butter in boxed meals. Use half the butter or margarine that's recommended in meals like Rice-a-Roni. Even better, skip the butter all together. You probably won't notice much difference and you'll spare yourself many hundred calories.

Heat the oil...Before sautéing anything in oil, make sure that a drop of water comes to an immediate boil if put in the oil. If it's not hot enough, the food will absorb more of the oil.

Turn the turkey upside down...When roasting turkeys or chicken, use a rack that will allow the fat to drip out of the bird. The racks, available in such specialty stores as Williams-Sonoma, help meats retain their flavor while reducing the fat content.

Steam...Use your steamer. Unlike most of the junk that usually ends up hidden in a closet, steamers can be an important part of a healthy diet. You'll cut out the fats used in sautéing or frying and will retain more of the vitamins. Studies indicate, too, that microwaved vegetables retain more vitamins than those that are boiled. So make it a habit to use healthier cooking methods.

Stroll before dinner. A quick stroll before dinner may act as an appetite suppressant so that you won't overeat. It will give your metabolism a boost to help you work off the night's calories.

Slice an onion. Don't chop. Chopping scatters the onion's stinging mist. Instead, glide the blade firmly through the onion as if through butter.

The sharper the knife, the gentler the sting. Rinse your hands after slicing an onion to avoid touching the oils to your eyes.

...Stick a straw in ketchup to make it easier to pour ...Store cottage cheese upside down to keep it fresh longer...Thaw frozen fish in milk to eliminate freezer odors

Broil with coals and bake with fire. When cooking over a campfire, use flames to boil water and bake bread. If you're going to fry up some bacon or trout, wait until the flames die down and use the coals.

Supplement your spaghetti sauce. Microwave fresh or frozen vegetables for a few seconds, then add them to bottled spaghetti sauce to improve both taste and the fiber and vitamin content of the sauce. Try carrots for beta carotene, bell peppers for vitamin C and fiber, or tomatoes for compounds that may help fight some forms of cancer.

Fill up before dinner. Try to eat the good stuff before you dig into the main course. Have, for example, both low-fat soup and salad before the main course. And drink down a big glass of water a few minutes before eating dinner. You'll trick your brain into thinking you're semi-full. The high fiber content and liquids will make you feel full so that you'll eat less Chicken Kiev.

Serve in the kitchen. Leave the bowls of stew or beanie weanie in the kitchen rather than bringing them to the table. You're less likely to go in for a fourth helping if it's not right there in your face.

Use chopsticks. Even if you're having, say, German food, try using chopsticks instead of a fork and knife. It will have the effect of slowing your consumption down, which means you'll eat less and digest better.

Eat an early dinner. It's a big mistake to eat a big meal before bed. Your body won't have time to metabolize the calories, so even a low-fat pasta dinner can store as body fat. Try to eat before 7:00 p.m.

Eat many fat fish...The omega-3 oils found in fish may cut your risk of heart disease by inhibiting the formation of blood clots. In areas of the world where fish is a staple, the rate of arte-

...Eat on white china to make even Hamburger Helper look classy
... Infuse garlic or herbs in your canola or olive oil...

riosclerosis seems to have been reduced, probably because the high consumption of fish oil has
increased the amount of plaque-fighting good
cholesterol in the blood. Fatty fish like salmon
and trout seem to work the best. Although sup-
plements are an option, it is not clear whether
they offer the same kind of efficacy as plain ol'
fish. The capsules also have the nasty side effect
of horrific, room-clearing fish burps. So stick
with a thick filet rather than a capsule.

And goats...Goat, which is one of the world's
favorite meats, has about half the fat of beef or
pork. Eat it instead of, say, a pork chop and you'll
be cutting your fat calories in half.

And buffalo. You like red meat. You will eat red
meat. So try buffalo (they're really American Bison,
but we've come to call these creatures "buffalo"),
which is a different animal altogether. It's deli-
cious, lean, and does not taste like chicken.

Remember the Japanese. They eat tofu. Women
there are one-third less likely to develop breast

cancer than in America. Men are less likely to develop prostate cancer. Arteriosclerosis is less common. A growing wealth of scientific literature indicates that tofu is near-medicinal in its health benefits. Perhaps it is the "phytoestrogens" or the lack of fat. We should all eat several servings of soy-based products like tempeh, soy milk, or tofu every day. It will be one of your best habits.

Stroll after dinner...A gentle walk after the evening meal will help you metabolize the calories you just consumed. But take it easy. You don't want to do any heart-pounding aerobics that could adversely effect your sleep. Remember to wear bright clothing if you're going to be out after dark. Carry a small flashlight to increase your visibility to drivers. Walk against traffic so that you can see approaching cars. Avoid looking at on-coming lights, which can momentarily blind pedestrians.

And remember the post-prandial papaya. Papain, the enzyme found in papaya, is a potent aid to digestion because of its ability to dissemble proteins. So have a piece of the fruit for desert. Not only is it a healthy alternative to ice cream, you'll get the added benefit of better digestion. Pick a papaya as you would a peach: the flesh should give to the touch, but not be too soft.

"He was a bold man that eat the first oyster."
JONATHAN SWIFT

Have a chaser when chugging sliders. To prevent a possible intestinal upset, follow up a raw oyster with a considerable slug of wine, beer or spirits. The alcohol may help kill off any stray bacteria if the oyster has headed south.

...Eat brown rice instead of white because it has more fiber and nutrients...Use olive oil instead of butter because of its ability to up the good cholesterol...Buy fish on the day you'll be eating it to help insure freshness...Eat no more than nine cheeseburgers per week...Eat angel food cake, which has no fat, for dessert, but do not top it with Chunky Monkey...

Use molasses. This dark brown syrup is a by-product of the sugar refining process. Unlike white sugar, molasses has some nutritional value, including iron and calcium. Use it as a sweetener instead of sugar. Or try sweetening food with chunks of apple instead.

Drink your milk. As you sleep, your body may leech calcium from bones to stabilize blood calcium levels. A glass of milk (or a calcium supplement) can help bolster calcium blood levels. This is especially important for women, who risk osteoporosis in later life. Men, too, should down a glass of non-fat milk to increase bone strength. And you know, of course, that milk can help you sleep. Buy milk in cardboard cartons rather than plastic. Milk that's stored in opaque plastic containers can lose much of its flavor and up to seventy percent of its vitamin A in a single day because of exposure to the grocery store's fluorescent lights. Try drinking your skim milk from a chilled glass. For reasons that shall forever remain unknown, it makes it taste more like whole milk.

And remember to chew your food. If you don't, who will?

Don't worry so much about fat

*"People very commonly complain of indigestion.
How can it be wondered at, when they seem by their
habit of swallowing their food wholesale, to forget
for what purpose they are provided with teeth?"*

From *ENQUIRE WITHIN UPON EVERYTHING*
a 19th century book of good habits

8

Be a Jock

*"I swing big, with everything I've got. I hit big or
I miss big. I like to live as big as I can."*
BABE RUTH

Bunt strikes, not balls.

Lay out the sweats. Prepare your exercise clothes
before you go to sleep as a not-so-subtle reminder to take a run before work. Make a thrice-
weekly appointment with yourself to exercise
and keep the appointment. You need to reinforce
the notion that exercise is not just a hobby but a
vital part of your day. Try to ingrain the routine.
Remember, too, that exercise should be energiz-

ing, not draining. If you find that, after a work-out and a shower, you feel sapped, then cut back on your routine. You can always build up slowly to a more intense workout. If exercise is making you tired, you'll probably stop. Studies have shown that there's no real benefit to exercising more than five days a week. So take it easy.

Wake up with the sun. Studies have shown that a good dose of rays in the morning helps sup-press the production of melatonin, a hormone that's responsible for sleepiness. So if weather permits, get outdoors as soon as possible after waking up. A bit of sun helps re-set your biolog-ical clock so that you can start the day with a solar flare. And stretch your muscles before ris-ing. It will help wake you up, and if you're stiff it'll make you feel better. Once stretched, try doing a few sit ups. Then reach for a glass of water to rehydrate—before you down a cup of coffee.

Imagine your workout. Before heading off to the gym or onto the track, play a mental movie of the workout in your head. Imagine the form you'll use, how your body will look, and the sweat running down your face. Athletes say such visualizations increase the productivity of both training and competition.

Crumple the morning paper. Take the Sports section in one hand and scrunch it into a ball. Then squeeze the ball and hold it for three seconds. Do this twenty-five times for each hand and you'll strengthen arm muscles and help stave off elbow injuries.

Get sloshed. Drink water before exercise. Try to down about sixteen ounces of water two hours before exercising. This will hydrate your system, and allow time for you to urinate before exercising. Drink as you exercise. Studies show that if you lose just two percent of your weight in water, your performance will drop twenty percent. So sip as you go.

Be a warm human being... Take six to ten minutes to warm your muscles before exercising. At rest, roughly eighty-five percent of your blood is in your torso. Warming up redistributes your blood to the muscles where it's needed for exercise. Sports physicians recommend doing a slow-motion version of whatever exercise you'll be performing as your main aerobic activity. For example, if you jog, jog very slowly until your body temperature rises. Although stretching is also a vital part of exercise, remember to warm up *before* you stretch so that your muscles have a good supply of blood.

And then count to thirty—about how long it takes for a muscle to release its tension. So give it half a minute when loosening up those hamstrings. If you don't stretch for thirty seconds, it may do little good. Remember not to bounce during a stretch. Just bring the muscle to the point of tension and hold it. Try to stretch it progressively further as it loosens up.

Put a top spin on the spike...When playing volleyball, make it a habit to snap your wrist when spiking. This should put an impressive top-spin on the ball, which will make it difficult to return. When serving, hit the center of the ball with the heel of your hand.

Keep score...As one writer notes, keeping detailed score at a baseball game "burns the play into memory." It also increases your knowledge of the game and brings you closer to the action. So grab a score card as you enter the stadium and follow the game both with your eyes and a number two pencil.

And scan for cat's paws. When sailing in light air, scan the water for small ripples that indicate the presence of wind. Inform the helmsman that you've found some cat's paws. It will be welcome news.

Set realistic goals. Hiking the length of the John Muir trail within a month from today is unrealistic; adding a mile for every month of jogging is both challenging and do-able. Set your sights high, but not too high. Then achieve your goals.

Work out between 4:00 and 7:00 p.m. Many sports physiologists feel that this is the optimum time for athletic performance. Your body temperature has started to rise from its afternoon slump, so you'll have energy. Any later than 7:00 p.m. and you'll be too wired to sleep well. The morning is a good time to exercise as well, but most of us just don't really feel like it. So try the late afternoon.

Hold a baseball with the fingertips...Don't cram the ball into your hand, but caress it as if made of crystal. Use your fingertips and you'll improve both control and velocity. If you want the ball to sink, lay your fingers in the same direction as the ball's threads. If you want the ball to rise, put them across the seam.

And chalk the cue, don't cue the chalk. When playing pool, apply chalk to the tip of the cue before every shot. Always go for the easiest shot.

Run or walk...You don't need a gym or any fancy overpriced home equipment except for tennis shoes (which you should buy on sale). You don't have to compete with anybody but yourself. And you don't have to contend with the crowds at the gym. You'll have very few excuses to miss a workout.

But walk *right*. Walking has become one of America's leading exercises. Although you should walk in a way that feels most comfortable, there are a few guidelines to get the most from a stroll: Keep you head held high, with your chin parallel to the ground. Keep your stomach pulled in to avoid strain on your back. Swing your arms in opposition to the stride of your feet. Keep your step light, rather than slamming your feet down on the ground. Walk at a good clip—more than three miles per hour—for the greatest cardiovascular benefits. This advice holds true whether you're out for a heart-pumping bit of exercise or just going to the convenience store for a carton of milk. And bend. When walking or hiking downhill, keep knees slightly bent. This reduces the strain that can cause injury and soreness from downhill hikes. Take a vigorous walk three or four times a week for forty-five minutes and you meet your aerobic exercise requirements.

> *"In walking, it is necessary to bear in mind that the locomotion is to be performed entirely by the legs. Awkward persons rock from side to side helping forward each leg alternately by advancing the haunches. This is not only ungraceful but fatiguing."*
> FROM *ENQUIRE WITHIN UPON EVERYTHING*

...Take the stairs, not the elevator...Walk the airport when delayed...Put a can or two in your knapsack when on a day hike.

Get off early. When taking a bus (which you should do often), get off a few stops early for a good morning walk. Although most of us think we need a heart-pumping, sweat-inducing workout, new research indicates that exercise is *cumulative.* A few hundred yards here and there during the course of the day could add up to a five-mile hike.

Run before you lift. To improve the duration of your workout, studies suggest that we should do aerobics (walking, running, bicycling) before we do weight work. If you lift weights first, it's likely that your muscles will be too tired to do much else. If your workout includes both, do the heart-pounding exercise before the back-breaking exercise.

Waggle. Before striking a golf ball, take a few practice swings and settle into position by waggling, or moving the club near the ball while making a few body motions of your choice. It will help you focus and relax. Make it a habit to become composed before undertaking any athletic endeavor. Waggling is just one example of what jocks can do to center themselves before exercise or competition.

"Golf is a good walk spoiled."
MARK TWAIN

Practice…Make disciplined training one of your important habits. You'll never achieve mastery—whether it be the piano, archery or a good chip shot—if you do not hone the skill through rigorous practice.

Exaggerate…Use exaggerated motions as a way of better understanding a sport. For example, exaggerate the motion of shooting a free-throw and you may find that you'll gain control over the shot. Over-swing through a golf ball and you may see what you're doing wrong. Exaggeration is a useful technique used by trainers in many different sports.

Daydream...Think about that mountain cabin, or winning the lottery, or doing laundry. Let your mind wander a bit and you may stay on the bike for ten more minutes.

And focus on perfection. Keep a mental image of the perfect form for the exercise and then do it. A bicep curl, for example, should be done slowly and evenly, with as much emphasis given to putting the weight down as lifting it up. Every exercise—including running—has a form to it. So keep an image of that perfect form in your mind's eye. It will help your performance.

Stare at the ceiling...When doing sit-ups, isolate your stomach muscles by focusing on the ceiling. Or try pushing your tongue against the roof of your mouth for the same effect. Try doing a few sit-ups before getting out of the bed in the

...Try one new sport every year... When running to catch a baseball, make sure everyone knows as much by yelling "Mine!" or "I've got it!" Remember to keep your eyes on the ball

morning to give yourself that much more tone. Forget the hundreds (thousands?) of abdominal machines on the market. All you need, according to experts, is a floor upon which to do well-executed, conventional sit-ups.

Keep your hands on the rail...Don't grab the rail when using a step machine. Not only will you increase the difficulty of your workout by some twenty-five percent, you'll also avoid the back and neck strain that comes from crouching over the machine. It's estimated that you use seven percent *fewer* calories for every ten pounds of weight supported by the rails.

...Do ten push-ups during commercial breaks to increase muscle tone...Snap the wrist when skimming rocks on water...

Bike to a beat...Researchers have found that listening to music while exercising can keep the rider on the bike or treadmill for as much as twenty-five percent longer. So invest in a Walkman and shoot for your target heart rate.

And practice the "explosive exhale." Marathon runners have a little trick they use when pushing the envelope of endurance. They take a deep breath and blow it out with as much force as they can muster. It's called the "explosive exhale" and it helps many endurance athletes find inspiration during a rough patch. Try it when you feel as if you can't work out anymore. It works during sex, too.

Use the mirror... Avoid scales as a measure of progress. They may indicate whether or not you're losing weight, but they won't tell you whether it's fat, muscle or just water weight. Ideally, you want to increase your lean muscle mass while reducing the percentage of body fat. So it's possible to gain weight (muscle weighs more than fat) while getting into better shape. Use the mirror to see if your muscle tone and overall appearance have improved.

Change your program... When you've gotten into a good rhythm with your exercise, remember to adjust your program as you get stronger. Run a bit longer. Lift a bit more weight. Stay on the treadmill for a few more minutes.

And push the envelope. There's been a dramatic move away from the philosophy of "no pain, no gain," but there may come a time when you must push yourself to test the limits of your ability. The world would have missed its greatest athletic performances if folks like Kerri Strugg had not pushed the envelope. Be in great shape before you try.

And remember to breathe the same air but once...

> *"Air once breathed has lost the chief part of its oxygen,*
> *and acquired a proportionate of carbonic acid gas.*
> *Therefore, health requires that we breathe*
> *the same air only once."*
> From *ENQUIRE WITHIN UPON EVERYTHING*

9

Look Both Ways
Before Crossing

*"Do not stand in a place of danger
trusting in miracles."*
AN ARAB PROVERB

When out and about...

Dress Down...Thieves love to see the kind of ostentatious displays of wealth that can make their work so rewarding. So try to be moderate in your dress, especially when it comes to jewelry like Rolex watches. Avoid wearing Fabergé egg necklaces at all costs.

Act confident...Walk briskly, with head and shoulders held high. Criminals prefer a lack of confidence (slouching, staring at the ground) which can indicate easy prey. Act is if there's a string pulling your head and shoulders skyward. Do not make eye contact, but don't look away, either. Don't be cocky or tough, which may invite a challenge. Just go about your business with an air of self-possession.

Hide money. When wearing Levi's, for example, stick a twenty dollar bill in those tight little coin pockets that no one ever uses. If you get ripped off, you won't be left penniless.

And trust your instincts. If a situation gives you a feeling of uneasiness—a dark ATM, a quiet street—go with your gut. If you're wrong, then little is lost. If you're right, you may have put yourself out of harm's way.

When encountering a shark, make it a habit to swim away in slow, even strokes. Don't splash or panic. This will just make him salivate. If he does come in for a nosh, make it a habit to slug him in the snout with all your might. *Use* that nervous energy. If you have anything handy, try poking him in his beady little fish eyes.

Be ready to transact...Have all your automatic teller forms ready to go before you get out of your car. The less time at an ATM, the better. Only use ATMs that are well-lighted and in areas with plenty of foot traffic. Conduct business transactions briskly and efficiently to limit your exposure to the bad guys. This includes keeping tip money in your pocket. That way you won't have to pull out your wallet in a potentially dangerous setting.

Walk down the middle of the sidewalk. If you're near the curb, bad guys can get you from their car. If you're close to doors or alleys, the same can happen. So make like a politician and stick to the middle of the road.

Be prepared to push buttons...Stand near the elevator control panel. If another passenger accosts you in any way, push as many floor buttons as you can, along with the emergency button. If the criminal knows that the elevator will be stopping at every floor, he's less likely to do you harm.

Use a fanny pack instead of a purse. Thugs don't want to mess with anything that's hard to grab. If you must wear a purse, sling it over your head and at an angle to make it a harder target.

Then yell "Fire!" Your fellow citizens are more likely to react to a threat to their own safety then somebody else's. In any event, yelling "Fire!" will bring out the cavalry. This may not be a wonderful statement about man's concern for his fellow man, but it is an eminently practical habit.

When at home...

Pretend. When you hear an unexpected knock at the door, pretend to be talking on the phone. If the person possesses nefarious intent, he's less likely to follow through if he knows you're in communication with a friend. And, of course, always ask who it is that's knocking at your door.

Test batteries. In your smoke detectors, especially, once every month or two. But also in your flashlights, car alarm beepers, remote control gate openers...It could make a big difference in a dangerous situation.

Rip up applications. If you've declined one of those pre-approved credit cards, don't throw away the form. Instead, tear it into tiny bits. Criminals can use the codes on the form to rip off both you and the card company.

Buy shoes that feel comfortable from the start. Breaking in shoes can take a long time, and it may never happen. Your big toe should have plenty of wiggle room, and the heel should be snug but not tight. Or go barefoot, because an airing out of one's toes is not just good for the sole, but also helps fight bacteria. And walking barefoot helps develop a protective layer of calluses.

When caught in a tornado, make it a habit to go under a sturdy table in the center of the basement. In an earthquake, select a sturdy table away from windows.

Shovel safely. Take a vigorous warm-up and stretch before shoveling snow. Snow-shoveling is more deadly in this country than disgruntled postal workers, so be careful. Use a shovel that won't require deep bending. Let your legs do most of the work to prevent back strain. Dress in layers that you can peel off as you heat up from the work. Take frequent breaks, even if you're in good shape.

Wear earplugs. If you're mowing the lawn, practicing scales on the Les Paul, or sanding down the deck, use earplugs. It will help prevent any damage to your hearing.

Grip the rungs, not the side rails. When climbing a ladder, use both hands to grip the rungs rather than the rails. If you slip, you can grab the next rung rather than sliding all the way down. Set the base out one foot for every four feet of height.

Freeze. If attacked by a Grizzly bear in your home, make it a habit to stay put. These bad boys can reach forty miles per. You can't. If you have friends over for cocktails, stand together and wave your arms like some weird crab. That should scare the bejeezus out of the poor bear. If he gets real close, play dead. This should not be a habit with black bears, however, because black bears like to eat dead things.

While abroad...

Park a car. When you're on vacation, get a friend or neighbor to park his or her car in your driveway.

Have them pick up the newspapers, open or close your curtains on occasion, and perhaps turn on the television for a few hours. If you can, forward calls to a friend in case the bums have your home phone. Burglars don't like signs of inhabitancy.

Imagine. When flying, go over the plane's escape route with eyes closed. Imagine that you have to crawl to the emergency exits in the dark. Visualize what you'd do to get there and how to open the hatch.

Tell the cops. When you leave for a long while, notify local police. They'll usually make a point to keep tabs on your property.

Administer Coca-Cola. When stung by a jelly fish in an exotic locale, make it a habit to pour a coke on the sting. Coca-Cola is available in places of great wealth and utter famine, and should thus follow you wherever you may travel. It will help neutralize the poison and, as you writhe in pain, may even remind you of home. We understand that generic cola works just as well.

Remove the winch handle. When trimming the sails on a sailboat, remember to remove the winch handle from the winch when finished. If it remains, you might fall into it and crack a rib. Remember, even if you never set foot on a sailboat, to be aware of your environment and the dangers therein. And, like a winch handle, either remove the danger or yourself.

Refer to Polaris. If you become unsure of your direction, make it a habit to seek out the North Star. First find the Big Dipper. Then run an imaginary line from the two stars on the outer edge of the dipper. They will lead you to Polaris. You will be looking towards true north.

Put the key where you know it'll be. Whether you're at a Motel Six in Bakersfield or the Oriental in Bangkok, keep your hotel key in the same spot whenever you travel (for example, on top of the television). You won't lose precious seconds looking for it in case you have to leave quickly. A few other habits for safe hotel stays: locate the fire stairs on your floor and then make note of the distance (in steps) from your room to the exit door. Do the same with the fire alarm. Read your room's safety directions when you first arrive. It's doubtful you'll stop to study them as your room fills with acrid black smoke.

Extricate yourself from a python's death grip. If you find yourself wrapped in a mortal coil by a large boa constrictor while visiting Africa, make it a habit to extricate yourself from your plight. Remember that when unwrapping a constrictor, it is best to begin at the tail, not at the head. The reptile won't be able to put up as much of a fight if you begin at its end rather than its beginning. If you start at his head, you'll just make him testy.

While operating a motor vehicle...

Take emergency provisions. When traveling by car in winter, make it a habit to take along the following items: A blanket, flashlight, canned food, chocolate bars, bottled water, flares, and jumper cables. Add whatever else you may think of to increase your sense of safety and comfort when buried under tons of dangerously shifting snow.

*"I always keep a supply of stimulant handy in case
I see a snake. I always keep a snake handy, as well."*
W.C. FIELDS

*...Keep kitty litter in
your trunk to use
for traction when
stuck in the mud*

Keep it quarter-full. Don't let your car's gas tank
get less than a quarter full. If you keep it at least
quarter-full, there will be no chance of running
into trouble after running out of gas.

Get wired. If you're even the slightest bit sleepy
before a long drive, then have a cup or two of
Joe. Better to lose sleep later than end up ca-
reening over a precipice. Or just don't drive
when tired.

Pre-program. If you use a cell phone while driving, pre-program the numbers you'll be calling
during your drive. A recent study found that
driving while talking on a cell phone is as dangerous as driving drunk. With that startling an-
nouncement in hand, it's best to have numbers
pre-programmed so you will fiddle with your
phone as little as possible. Better yet, just listen
to the radio.

Keep car windows cracked. When you're on a long road trip, keep your windows open just a bit to help you stay awake. Many highway accidents happen because of drowsiness. A bit of cool (or even cold) air will keep you alert.

Leave a space. When stopped at a light, allow a car length between you and the next car. If someone attempts to rob or car-jack you, there will be room to swerve around and drive off. And stay in the center lane. It makes it harder for a potential car-jacker to jump from the curb towards your door.

... Wear goggles while playing racquetball, a helmet for biking, and joint pads for roller-skating ... Wear sun-glasses with good U.V. protection ...

Stretch before unloading. After a long car journey, make sure to relax and stretch before grabbing a suitcase from the trunk. Your muscles will be cold, and you'll risk injury if you don't stretch. A sore back can put a crimp in your vacation.

Soak your clothes. It is a myth that you can survive in the desert by drinking your own urine (or anyone else's). It will only increase thirst and dehydration. And you'll end up with terrible pee-pee breath. But urine does come in handy. If, while on a relaxing drive through one of our great desert regions, you find yourself stuck in the heat of the day, make it a habit to soak your clothes in urine to stay cool. This is a very real (albeit unpopular) survival tactic employed by outdoor types.

Tip them, but don't trust them. Give the valet only your car keys. No house keys, no ID. Nothing. While you're at dinner, the friendly valet can note your address and copy your keys.

Aim forward. When parked in a driveway, try to point the front of the car toward the sidewalk so that a would-be thief will have an audience to contend with. Always set your parking brake and turn your wheels hard in one direction. This makes it very difficult for anyone thinking of ripping off your car with a tow truck (don't laugh—it happens more often than you think).

And don't forget to check the back seat...

10

Kick

"I never smoked a cigarette until I was nine."
H.L. MENCKEN

Oversmoke. When smoking, take a puff every five to seven seconds. It'll make you sick and help you stop. And brush your teeth immediately after dinner to quash the desire for a smoke.

Tear it in half. Smoke only half of each cigarette. You'll get the dose of nicotine your addicted body craves, but you'll reduce the damage each cigarette can do to your precious self by halving the amount of nicotine and, more importantly, the tar that your lungs receive.

Make it illegal. Hang out in the no-smoking section. Go to restaurants, theaters, bookstores—anywhere where smoking is verboten—to pass the time.

Limit the number. Buy cigarettes by the pack, not the carton. If they're not around the house, your will power will be all the greater. If they are around, you'll probably grab them like a lifesaver in the ocean. Keep a tally of the staggering amount of money you save and spend it on a pair of jogging shoes.

Maintain a visual aid. Keep a jar of your smoked butts on the bed next to you. It's a truly disgusting display of your habit. It may help you realize what you're putting into your lungs. Or try smoking with the wrong hand in front of a mirror to make you realize how stupid you look.

11

Get your ZZZZZZZs

*"The bed has become a place of great
luxury to me. I would not exchange it
for all the thrones in the world."*
NAPOLEON

Worry *before* you go to bed. Try going somewhere other than the bedroom to stew for about
fifteen minutes before retiring. It's a way of clear-
ing out those angst-ridden pipes of yours so that
you can get a good night's sleep. Want to poison
your boss? Plan it in the dining room, not the
bedroom. Angry at your boyfriend? Throw darts
in the bathroom. The worst time to dwell on
your troubles is at about 3:00 a.m. Better to set

aside a special, private time for high anxiety and neurosis rather than ruin your sleep.

Be ritualistic. Read a book. Take a bath. Walk the dog. Do whatever rituals you do to tell yourself that it's beddy-bye time. It is a simple, effective way of winding down for both children and adults.

Eat carbos at night. It's a delicate balance—eat carbohydrates such as brown rice with a little protein and you've got an energy-providing combination that is likely to keep you awake. But if you eat a big plate of pasta with no protein (and on an empty stomach), the result will likely be sleepiness. Carbohydrates increase the output of serotonin, a brain chemical that causes, among other things, relaxation and drowsiness. This effect lessens or is even negated in the presence of protein. So eating a big load of starches for dinner can help you fall asleep. Try baked potatoes, which digest quickly.

Get up early. Rising early—no matter how weary you may be—is the best assurance for a good night's sleep. And it has been said that rising early may even make you healthy, wealthy and wise.

Remember what the bed is for. It is one of humanity's great inventions, but its uses are limited. To improve your sleep, limit your time in bed to sleep, sex, and a few minutes of late-night reading. Once you begin to associate your mattress with work matters, or phone calls, or newspapers, then it may lose its association with sleep. That, in turn, can keep you from slumber. Don't get into bed until tired. Don't lie there for more than fifteen minutes in an attempt to sleep. If you're not snoozing within fifteen minutes, get up and sit in a comfortable chair until you're ready to try again.

III

*Putting One's
Home in a
Semblance of Order*

12

Watch the Clock

"We kill time; time buries us."
JOAQUIM MARIA MACHATO DE ASSIS

Do what's important to you. Make a list of the elements of your life that have the most meaning. What does it include? Your spouse, your children? Career advancement? Daytime television? Now make a list of how you really spend your time in the course of the day. Do the two match up? Try to taper back on the activities that have little or no meaning—watching re-runs of "The Price is Right," for example. Spend your free time, if you have any, participating in an activity that has some real value: A cup of coffee with a friend you haven't seen in some time. Planting a tree. Teaching your child how to tie a square knot. Learn to make the most of time. Learn, too, to waste time with great verve.

Plan your day. Sit down every morning and spend ten minutes writing up a list of things you'd like to accomplish. These few minutes could save an hour or two of needless effort. When making appointments—with doctors, hair stylists, dentists—always try to book the first slot to avoid the inevitable back-ups that occur as the day goes on. Always call ahead to see if your doctor is running on time so that you can avoid the frustration of a waiting room.

Lay out your clothes. Do your morning chores the night before. Pick out the suit you plan to wear tomorrow. Get your coffee ready to perk. Organize your briefcase while watching television. Do whatever you can in advance the night before to insure that you won't be rushed in the morning.

Make appointments with yourself. Treat your busy times like an important appointment with a client. And keep the appointment. It will keep bothersome interruptions from getting in the way of your work.

Practice the art of multiplicity. Do multiple tasks at the same time. Fold laundry while watching "Baywatch." Pay your bills in the dentist's waiting room. Do three dishes while microwaving. Make it a habit, in short, to free up time by using a few seconds here and there to accomplish the small tasks that fill up our days. It will give you more time for matters of significance.

Cluster errands together...It is a big waste of time to make three trips when one will do. If you need to shop, go to the bank and the post office as well; schedule a time in the day when you can accomplish all three on one circuit. Keep a "To Buy" list on your refrigerator to avoid duplicate trips to the market. Not only does it save time, but it cuts down on gas consumption and reduces pollution.

And group like tasks together. If you've got thirty items on your to-do list, group them by similarity. For example, lump phone calls with phone calls, memos with memos, and meetings with meetings. You will not only save time, but will reduce the list of thirty to five lists of six—a cheap, but effective psychological ploy to reduce stress. You're then better able to prioritize the tasks. Cross items off the list as you go to avoid wasting the time it takes to re-read them.

Cut office visits short. When someone enters your office for no good reason, stand up from your chair and say "What can I do for you?" It's a pleasant way of saying, "This better be important." It sends a distinct message that now is not the time for a casual chat. Try avoiding eye contact as people walk by your office to discourage such drop-ins.

Screen calls. This is the beauty of technology. One can have a lovely dinner and not have to jump up to answer a call from the Democratic fund-raiser or a new credit card offer. Use your answering machine early and often. Return calls during unproductive times of the day. Even better, just unplug the phone for a few hours.

Reply on the letter. Write a quick, handwritten note in the corner of the very letter you just received. It's much faster than typing out a formal letter. Obviously, this is not appropriate in all cases, but it's often fine. And it saves paper.

Call just before quitting time. People are less likely to keep you on the phone gabbing when they're eager to get home to their martinis. Or try calling just before lunch, when people are eager to rush out for their martinis. If you get an answering machine, tell it your business and then, if applicable, say "no need to call back." This will save both you and the callee the wasted time of an unnecessary conversation.

Leave the office. If you're overwhelmed by impromptu conferences and never-ending phone calls, just get out. Go to a local coffee shop and do your work over a double mocha. The one caveat here is that you must be more productive out of the office than in it. Otherwise you will be thought of as a slacker.

"So little time, so little to do."
OSCAR LEVANT

...Make sure your flight is not behind schedule before leaving home...Use free grocery delivery services...Listen to language tapes while stuck in rush hour traffic to make use of wasted time...

Use your *TV Guide*...You may have thought that picking up the *TV Guide* would mean that you were a confirmed TV junkie. You should, in truth, read the TV listings to see if there's anything on *worth* watching. Once the TV's on, it's usually on for many hours. If you don't find anything, then do something more productive (which includes every other human activity). If there is something on you'd like to watch, don't turn on the TV until the show starts, and turn it off when it's over.

Use your VCR...Tape your favorite shows and watch them without commercials. It cuts the show by a third, and may also make it conform to your schedule a bit better. Treat television like junk food, which is great in moderation, but you wouldn't want to eat it four or five hours a night.

Or just turn it off. Pick one day a week and make it a television-free zone. No TV on the Sabbath. Or another day of your choosing. Imagine how much you could accomplish if you pursued your ambitions during the time you now spend watching television.

Back yourself into a corner. Make a promise to finish a project by a certain date. Or plan to discuss a book next Tuesday. Make it impossible to procrastinate. This may not be relaxing, but it will help you to organize your time and accomplish your goals.

Shop by mail. Call the catalog company's 800-number during off-hours to insure you'll get through without a busy signal. With 24-hour-a-day numbers, call after 10:00 p.m.

"I must say I find television very educational. The minute somebody turns it on, I go to the library and read a good book."
GROUCHO MARX

Cook in bulk. Bake eight potatoes instead of just one. Keep the others in the fridge. Make six cups of rice and use plastic bags to freeze what you don't use. It cuts down on cooking time and saves on gas bills. You're also more likely to make good dietary choices if something healthy is already waiting for you in the fridge. If you don't feel like cooking eight potatoes, then at least cook for tomorrow by doubling what you'll need for tonight.

Keep tickets in your wallet... Keep laundry and dry cleaning stubs with you instead of at home so that you can stop by the cleaners whenever it's most convenient.

And soapy water in the sink. Do dishes right after you use them, or while cooking. It keeps dishes from accumulating, which can cut down on dish-cleaning later. And wipe up spills before they harden. A person who's pressed for time shouldn't worry too much about a spotless house. Just do the minimum it takes to be presentable— throw back the covers rather than making the bed, do the dishes and vacuuming. If you've got guests coming over, don't go nuts trying to make your house look like Martha Stewart has been doling out advice. Just be tidy. If your house is not as clean as you'd like it to be, but a friend is about to arrive, try putting out some flowers— your friend will be less likely to notice the mess.

And remember to...

> *"Never put off until tomorrow*
> *what you can do*
> *the day after tomorrow."*
> MARK TWAIN

13

Make Your Bed

"Clean your rooms well, for good spirits will not live where there is dirt. There is no dirt in heaven."
MOTHER ANN, *founder of the Shakers*

Change your clothes... If you're about to clean your house, change into grubby rags. Besides the obvious benefit of preserving your better garments, it's also an effective psychological ploy to put you in a scrubbing and sweeping frame of mind. Old clothes will probably keep you on the job longer.

Know from whence it came. Have a place for everything in your house, and put everything in its place. Cleaning a house is much quicker and easier if you know where things should go. If, on the other hand, you choose to pile stuff on the nearest flat surface (a table, a chair), the house will soon be overflowing. If you know immediately where to store all your possessions, then clean-up will go about five times faster. So put it where it belongs. Establish a place—a drawer, a box, an entire garage—for every item you own. It is, simply, easier to be organized than disorganized. While it may seem that messy is easier than tidy, the truth is that messy is much more work. Remember, though, that cleaning and organizing are separate and distinct. So don't try to arrange a closet at the same time you're cleaning it.

Clean downward... Start at the top of, say, a closet, and work your way down. The dust and gunk will fall towards the bottom, which can then be vacuumed up. If you work from the top down, you get an assist from gravity.

Take it one drawer at a time. The battle against clutter is on-going. But try not to think in terms of your entire house. Do a single drawer or file folder at a time lest you become overwhelmed.

Think seasons. Why keep thermal underwear in the drawer in spring? Keep seasonal stuff (Christmas ornaments, diving masks) in sturdy banker's boxes in the attic or basement until needed. Mark them carefully so you don't have to waste time searching for the item come summer. This can also include the rarely-used fondue set or Soloflex that do little more than take up space. Go through the house with a critical eye and you'll be surprised at how much more room you have once you stow away the non-vital property.

Use but a single chair. We all throw coats, purses and magazines on chairs in the misbegotten hope that they will one day migrate to their rightful home. This does not happen. So designate just *one* chair in your home for such duty (or perhaps two if you live in a multi-story place). You'll still possess the God-given right to throw your clothes around, but when you decide to put them away it will make clean-up much faster if the clothes are centrally located.

Fill gaps. Use the area between appliances for storage. Trays and cans might go between the stove and cabinet. Perhaps there's room beside your refrigerator for a broom. Use every avail-

Roll your towels. Try rolling towels rather than folding them. It saves a great deal of space. And it looks very cool.

able space in your home rather than leaving flotsam where it doesn't belong.

Use two buckets. Keep the soapy water in one, and rinse the dirty mop in the other. Your mop stays clean and your floors get cleaner because you're not using dirty cleaning water.

> *"Cleanliness prevents the pernicious effects of dampness,*
> *of bad smells, and of contagious vapors arising*
> *from substances abandoned to putrefy."*
> From ENQUIRE WITHIN ABOUT EVERYTHING

Throw it away...If copies of a given document exist somewhere else, dump it. This applies to magazines, newspapers, bills, legal documents and correspondence. Try to also get rid of early drafts of projects that are now complete, unless of course those early drafts contain ideas you may want to go back to later.

Throw it away right away. When going through old clothes, books or junky items, give them to Goodwill that very day. Don't let them sit in a

...Keep the shower curtain inside the tub ...Fold clothes as they come out of the dryer to avoid wrinkling...Do your dishes before you go to sleep because it's depressing to wake up to a sink full of pots and pans

corner while you have time to change your mind. Throw away anything that's not useful or beautiful or both.

Swap new clothes for old. Give away one or two older garments every time you buy a new piece of clothing. You'll find that you probably have drawers full of garments that you haven't touched in two or three years.

Empty file folders. Every time you open a file folder, try to dispose of some of the paper therein. Don't make a big project of it—just a sheet or two every time. Try to keep the file less than six inches thick.

Save the article, not the magazine. Sure, you want to finish that story in the *New Yorker* about how the hormonal balance of every human on earth has been thrown out of whack by pollution. But do you really need the entire issue? Keep a pair of scissors handy. Clip articles you want to read later, and stick them into a folder

...Use Play-Doh to remove grime from your computer keyboard...Read your mail over the recycling box and dump the junk as soon as your eyes scan over it. Be liberal in your dumping...Put a drop of perfume on a light bulb to make the room smell purty...

right away. Dump anything you haven't gotten back to after three full moons.

Check the medicine chest. Throw away old drugs that have expired, including aspirin or acetaminophen, or capsules that are dried or cracked. Throw out any liquid medications that look cloudy or discolored, or chipped tablets and tubes that are cracked or leaky. This is not only a good de-cluttering habit. It's also good for your health.

Think of gifts like candy. Gifts can express a lovely sentiment, but that doesn't require you to keep them around for the rest of your life. Like flowers or bon-bons, some gifts start to take on a noxious odor after a few weeks. So get rid of them without regret. Take a picture, then dump it. If you insist that the sequin donkey from Ensanada is an important part of your emotional landscape, take a photograph. Then say *"Hasta la vista"* and throw it away. The same applies to all manner of souvenir and trinket that hold sway over you. Taking a picture is a good way of relieving the guilt you'll feel for trashing that gift from Uncle Sid.

Clean during this important message from our sponsors. Take the two minutes of commercial breaks to accomplish one small cleaning task: unload a dishwasher, tidy up a bed, fold a sweater or two, hang up some of your laundry.

Air out your shoes. To avoid both stink foot and fungus, give your shoes a chance to air out. Avoid wearing the same shoes two days in a row. Instead, loosen the laces and pull out the tongue. Putting them in fresh air will inhibit the grown of bacteria. As a twisted little aside, singer Madonna revealed to David Letterman that she has the singular habit of urinating on her feet while showering as a deterrent against athlete's foot. Is this a good habit? We leave the answer to you and your doctor. And we promise to make mention of urine only once more within the pages of this book.

Line the laundry. Use plastic garbage bags to line your clothes hamper. It will save time by making laundry easy to swoop out of the hamper. It will also keep down odors from mold and mildew in the hamper.

Segregate. Do socks with socks, underwear with underwear. If you do one type of apparel per load, you'll save time in folding and storing. It's helpful, too, to buy all white socks with the same kind of stripes or no stripe at all. Then you don't have to worry about sorting.

Season. Season cast iron pots and pans regularly. Rub a little oil into the pans and then put them into a warm oven for an hour or two to keep them in good shape. Do the same with woks.

Reward yourself after the task is done. Give yourself a treat after, say, waxing the kitchen floor or filing your taxes. Tell yourself that you don't get to go see a movie or have a plate of ribs until after the chore is finished.

14

Be Tight with a Buck

*"To live within limits, to want one thing,
or a very few things, very much and love them dearly,
cling to them, survey them from every angle,
become one with them—that is what makes the poet,
the artist, the human being."*

GOETHE

Step on it. Before you put a new toilet paper roll on a dispenser, step on it to put a crease in the cardboard roll. When you go to take paper from the roll, you'll have to pull off sheets one at a time rather than having it unwind. This may sound rather obsessive. But if we all did this it would save a few thousand trees every year. More important, it is likely that if you acquire the admittedly odd habit of stepping on rolls of toilet paper, you will likely find other, more socially acceptable ways to live simply and frugally.

Pay as little rent as possible...

"Advertising is the rattling of a stick inside a swill bucket."
GEORGE ORWELL

"I went to the woods because I wished to live deliberately, to front only the essential facts of life, and see if I could not learn what it had to teach, and not, when I came to die, discover that I had not lived."

HENRY THOREAU

Ask yourself if you really need it. Stuff does not matter. People matter. Ignore advertising. Ad execs are very good at creating desire for products, but the desire is not real. Think twice about whether you'll really use the "Ab-Electrocutor," or if it will just end up in your closet with similar merchandise. Don't treat shopping as a leisure activity. Buy because you need, not because you think it will fill an unnamed void. The satisfaction that comes from buying a thing is short-lived, but the consequences to the environment (and your pocket-book) are long-lasting.

Glean. Check with local farms in your area to see if they allow gleaning, an age-old practice of allowing people to pick over crops deemed unmarketable by the farmer. The produce is often fine, but perhaps blemished or slightly over-ripe. You may be able to pick a peck of peppers for a pittance.

Wear simple clothing...

Drive old cars. Perhaps not ancient, but how about buying a three-year-old version of your dream car instead of a brand new model? A car loses a high percentage of its value in the first two years, even as it retains most of its quality. Drive the car until the axle drops out and you'll probably save yourself tens of thousands of dollars.

"Fashion is a form of ugliness so intolerable that we have to alter it every six months."
OSCAR WILDE

Buy other people's junk. Go to garage sales (or yard sales if you're back East) not just for hidden treasures, but for day-to-day necessities such as cookware, clothing and tools. Be wary of thrift stores, which have become trendy and expensive in the last few years.

"A bank is a place where they lend you an umbrella in fair weather and ask for it back when it begins to rain."
ROBERT FROST

Be like Oseola. You may have read about Oseola McCarty, an elderly woman with a sixth-grade education who recently donated her life savings of $150,000 to the University of Southern Mississippi. Generous, to be sure. What's amazing is that Oseola saved the money from her work as a simple laundress—ten dollars here, twenty there. "The secret to building a fortune," she says, "is compounding interest. It's not the ones that make the big money, but the ones who know how to save who get ahead. You've got to leave your investment long enough for it to increase." So be like Oseola and put away every spare cent. Then, like her, be a benefactor.

Save up for it. Open special accounts for large purchases like cars or washing machines. Make regular deposits into the account rather than making payments on a credit card. Remember that the ability to defer gratification is a sign of maturity.

Invest your lottery money. Instead of buying lottery tickets—perhaps the worst bet ever invented by man, take the ten or twenty bucks you throw away per month and put it into a stock or mutual fund. You will, in twenty or thirty years, have the small fortune that a lottery promises but rarely delivers. Try to think of your savings account as an expense, not a luxury. Your savings won't grow if you put it at the bottom of the list.

Use your debit card. More and more businesses now accept debit cards, which automatically reduce your checking balance. Unlike credit cards, which can lead to an unpleasant surprise at the end of the month, debit cards will keep you within your means. They offer the convenience of credit cards without the bad habit of high-interest.

Bounce your balance. This takes a bit of work, but look for credit cards with special low-interest offers. Transfer your balance from high-interest credit cards to ones with lower interest. The offers are usually for just six months or a year, so be prepared to transfer again when the time comes. You can also barter with your existing card company to see if they'll lower your interest rate rather than lose your patronage.

Be self-sufficient...

"No one must rely upon the industry of others, or expect their charity."
CONFUCIUS

...Run lemons under hot water before squeezing to get more juice... Shop when you're rested, unrushed and alone to avoid pressure and impulse buying

Pay your mortgage twice a month. Instead of waiting until the end of the month to pay say, one thousand dollars on your mortgage, pay five hundred dollars in the middle of the month and five hundred dollars at the end. By reducing your balance by five hundred dollars for those two weeks, you will accrue less interest. If you do this every month, you can pay off your mortgage substantially faster and with much less of your money going to interest. The same is true of credit cards.

Be like the Amish. This religious sect believes that pride is a sin. Their crafts display a simple, unadorned (and entirely modest) beauty. They have the habit of fashioning their own small gifts to give to loved ones. So instead of filling up your credit cards, try making a small, hand-painted bookmark (you can even copy an Amish design), or something similar. You'll probably spend less time on it than you would searching for parking at the mall, and the gift will have much more meaning for the receiver.

Fly though Vegas. There are often special discounts to and from this city so reliant upon gamblers. You may want to fly through Vegas to save a few hundred dollars. But *do not* get off the plane.

Go if it's free. Check out local universities or museums for lectures or shows. You'll probably find quite a few topics that will interest you. It's better than paying $7.50 for a mediocre film. Or sitting home for re-runs. Try the local events section in your paper for listings.

Rent art. Check to see if your local museum or library loans out art. You can sometimes borrow a beautiful old print for three or four months without paying a dime. It's a great way to change your decor without changing your cash flow. One doesn't need to own a thing to find it beautiful.

Put a clean nail into potatoes before baking to reduce your gas bill. The nail's metal will transfer the oven's heat into the core of the spud. You'll reduce your cooking time by fifteen minutes. Or

...Save old toothbrushes to use for cleaning grout ...Wear aprons when cooking to save on cleaning bills ...Max out your 401 K...Donate with a check so you'll have a record...

try boiling them for ten or fifteen minutes before baking. Over the course of a year of potatoes, that's a lotta lettuce.

...Keep your trunk empty and tires inflated to get better mileage...Carry a single check for a single purchase to avoid impulse buying

Forget cover letters...When faxing, leave off the cover letter and instead just write a small note at the top of the first page. This saves time, paper and, perhaps, long-distance phone charges.

Send a note...Spend a half-hour writing a note (cost—thirty-two cents) rather than making that long distance call to West Virginia. It will save money and may be more intimate than a phone call.

And buy Christmas trees straight from the train. You can save up to twenty percent if you head down to the tracks in your city and buy them straight off the train car. You'll also give your kids and yourself a memorable experience. Or, buy live trees that cost more, but can be planted.

Fill up in the a.m.... Fill your car's gas tank as early in the morning as you can. In the cool of the early morning, the gas is at its most condensed state, so you'll be getting more combustion for the buck. If you wait until it's warm, then the gas has expanded and is less economical. Physics does occasionally come in handy in real life.

Push it... If your lawn is fairly small, use a push mower instead of one with an engine. The initial cost will be lower, of course. And you'll save on gas, keep the neighborhood cleaner and quieter, and get a good bit of exercise.

...Order drugs via mail to save up to thirty-five percent off pharmacy prices ...Get shoes re-heeled at first sign of wear to prolong their life...

And freeze it. Make your own frozen pops using weird molds and wooden sticks. Try freezing fresh-squeezed juice, left-over pudding, or canned peaches. In the words of Descartes, or someone else whose name cannot be recalled, "Anything that can be imagined can be frozen." You'll save money by not buying those big-city, store-bought pops.

Think twice. Be as generous as you can with your time and know-how, but not with your money. Friendships become strained when money changes hands. Think long and hard before loaning your buddy five hundred bucks because you may never see it again. If you must loan money to friends, make sure there is a formal re-payment schedule and that both sides understand the terms. Be willing to accept the consequences if you should never see a dime of the money.

...Make blocks of ice for the cooler by freezing water in milk cartons...Add vinegar to the dishwasher to make detergent go further

Barter. In this era of K-Marts and Price Clubs, many retailers are now willing to negotiate prices. There's no benefit to being cheap or greedy, but see if you can't get the store to knock fifteen percent off the cost of the computer. When bartering, try to be charming and sympathetic to the seller. Don't try it when the business is busy. You should also make it a habit to exchange your talents, whatever they may be, for other goods or services. You may be able to get an air conditioner in exchange for a paint job.

Shop off-hours. When you shop for big items like televisions or kitchen appliances, go when the store is least crowded. If you go on a busy Saturday afternoon, you're less likely to get thoughtful information from the sales person. You're also less likely to get a good bargain from someone who does not have time to barter. In the same vein, try to run appliances during off-hours, as well. Electric rates change throughout the day, so find the cheapest times (usually after 10:00 p.m.) and take advantage of them by running the dryer or dishwasher a bit later.

Offer half in cash. For most items bought at yard sales or through classified ads, try using the lure of cash-in-hand to get the buyer to give up the goods for half the asking price. They will often say yes, and if not, you've gotten into a good bargaining position.

Shop at farmer's markets. The proliferation of street-side farmer's markets means that we can buy fresher produce, usually at reduced rates. And you'll get a bit of exercise wandering through the stalls.

Buy in bulk. Beans, spices and pastas can all be had for song if you avoid fancy packaging and buy

...Use rug beaters instead of vacuums to save electricity ...Sew it instead of throwing it away ...Wash your car at home ...Buy generic...

non-perishables by the gallon instead of by the pint. You'll also save time, since you won't need to replace them so often. Buying in bulk at places like the Price Club is not only a good idea, but even sort of hip. And buy big. Instead of sending your kids or yourself off with an eighty-nine cent bag of chips, buy one huge bag and divvy them up into various ziplock bags (which you can rinse and re-use, of course). Remember that convenience is both overrated and over-priced.

Brown-bag-it. Make and take your own lunch to work or school. You'll save money, make better dietary choices, and save time by not waiting for your food. If you eat at pricey restaurants every day, this new habit could save you thousands of dollars.

And remember that...

> *"With money in your pocket,*
> *you are wise and you are handsome*
> *and you sing well, too."*
> YIDDISH PROVERB

15

Work Hard

"I do not like work even when someone else does it."
MARK TWAIN

Be like Mother Ann. The woman who helped found the Shaker sect in the late 1700s found no real distinction between work and worship; hard work was not only a path to salvation, but salvation itself. Thus Shakers, who lived communally, rose at 4:00 a.m. and worked in their agrarian communes for over twelve hours a day. They believed that their work was nothing less than the outward extension of their souls. The result is some of the most elegant, functional and beautiful craftsmanship ever produced. So be like

Mother Ann and embrace your work. If you can do that, then the rest is easy.

Smile. Always be upbeat and optimistic at the office. That's not to say that you need to act as if you're in a Disney movie, but it's not going to do your career any good to seem mad or unhappy or exhausted. Even if you feel lousy, it's best to smile anyway.

Act confident even when you don't feel confident...

"To be a great champion you must believe you are the best. If you're not, pretend you are."
MUHAMMAD ALI

Focus on your strengths...It takes confidence to succeed, so remember the skills at which you excel and take pride. But don't be afraid to be afraid. Remember the first time you skied? Made love? Spoke in public? If you're never afraid, then you're probably not trying very hard. When you're afraid, just remember your strengths, marshal your talents and focus on the task ahead.

Speak up...Let your boss know what you want. Your superiors will have no idea how ambitious and energetic you are until you tell them. If you're craving a new position, or want a place on an exciting new project, you've got to speak up.

Take your boss' advice...It's not only good politics. You should also consider the possibility that she may know what she's talking about. It's tempting to think that you know more about your job than your superior, but try to heed her advice nonetheless.

And empower your employees. Let those beneath you choose tactics and implementation on their own. You'll develop a sense of team unity and bring out the best in your people.

Sell it one-on-one...If you've got an idea to pitch, approach the people who will be making the decisions on an individual basis. Lobby them directly rather than in the context of a meeting. Then bring up the idea in a formal meeting. You'll already have laid the ground work.

Volunteer to lead. Take on projects that no one else wants, like organizing a blood drive at work or the arrangements for a going-away party. Do a good job and you will be noticed. There are countless stories of low-level employees who rise

And be
flexible...

"A rigid army won't win; an inflexible tree will break. The unyielding and strong shall be brought low. The supple and delicate will rise above."
Huanchu Daoren

to executive positions after taking charge of an unpopular task.

Take sincere criticism with equanimity...

And learn from the opposition...

"It is said that someone who acts as an enemy toward you is your best teacher."
THE DALAI LAMA

"When a wise man is advised of his errors, he will reflect on them and improve his conduct. When his misconduct is pointed out, a foolish man will not only disregard the advice but rather repeat the same error. A man who is pleased when he receives good instruction will sleep peacefully, because his mind is thereby cleansed."
BUDDHA

But ignore critics...

"A crowd of savages, with knowledge or instinct enough to let them make the instruments speak, might have produced such noises."
Reaction to IGOR STRAVINSKY'S *Rite of Spring*

Work like Albert Einstein. The father of modern physics had three simple habits that guided his work, and may help guide yours as well. They are as follows: 1) Find simplicity in chaos; 2) Find harmony where there is discord; and 3) Find opportunity amidst difficulty.

Imagine the finished project. Try to visualize the project when it's complete. Imagine that the work is finished and, for whatever reason, you're merely copying over what you've already accomplished. This can sometimes build confidence when facing a daunting task.

And sweat the little stuff...

"Trifles make perfection, but perfection itself is no trifle."
A Shaker proverb

Break it down...Disassemble big tasks into a series of smaller tasks. You can usually take a project that seems overwhelming and break it down into a series of incremental steps. Focusing on smaller tasks usually makes one more productive. The difficult may seem less so once you take the first step. And make it a habit to be non-linear: Don't assume that you must begin at the beginning. Perhaps you'll need to write the conclusion to a report to understand the tone you want to communicate. Decide what works best for you.

Talk it out. If you're in the midst of a difficult project and can't find your way out, make it a habit to talk it out with friends and colleagues. They may be able to offer a simple fix to your problem. Or, through talking, you may find the solution yourself.

Work fast, because beating a deadline with good work in hand is one of the best ways to solidify your position at the office... Stay a little late, get there a little early... Make the coffee once in a while...

Act. Always follow through on your ideas, even if it amounts to nothing. Then act again. This is the only road to success. Remember that, as a wise guy once said, you can't plow a field by turning it over in your mind.

Use good tools...

> *"When I first commenced to paint with oil, I thought every painting would be my last one, so I was not so interested. Then the requests commenced to come for this one and that one... I think I am doing better work than at first, but it is owing to better brushes and paint." Consider your work with great care... "I like to finish a painting and then study it for a week or ten days, most always see then where one can improve..."*
> GRANDMA MOSES

Practice the conservation of energy. Don't discuss your grand ideas with anyone until you've begun to act upon them, or even until you finish. It is axiomatic that the more you blab, the less energy you have to complete those plans. So conserve energy by keeping your mouth shut.

Do heavy lifting in the morning...Tackle your most challenging projects between 10:00 a.m. and noon. If you've had a good breakfast, your blood sugar levels should be optimum, which means your brain function is at its peak. After noon, blood sugar levels and body temperature may drop, which accounts for that familiar afternoon slump. Studies suggest that for most people, the morning is our most productive time. So make it count. Save the easy tasks, like opening mail and returning phone calls, for a time in the day when your energy is low. This is usually between 1:00 p.m. and 4:00 p.m. for most of us. But fix it in the afternoon. Most of us are, despite lagging energy, at our most coordinated in the afternoon. So do the things that require hand-eye agreement like carpentry or painting in the afternoon.

And finish well...

"In pursuing their affairs, people often fail when they are close to success. Therefore, if one is as cautious at the end as at the beginning, there will be no failures."
LAO TSE

Leave thy desk. It may be tempting to impress your boss by wolfing down a sandwich at your desk. But it's not good for you. Get out of the office and into the air during lunch. You'll come back refreshed, which is really what your boss wants. So take every break that's coming to you, and spend a full lunch hour outside the confines of your cubicle.

Do your homework. Get plenty of information before you reach a decision, especially when it's important to you and your career. Hear from both sides of the issue.

Make a stand at the office. Try making phone calls while standing instead of sitting. You'll find that it improves the timbre of your voice, which can come in handy during a business call. It also improves the quality of your breathing, which means you'll get more oxygen to your brain.

Eat away your slump. If your energy lags before an afternoon meeting, try a light snack of lean protein (yogurt, cottage cheese) and a piece of fruit. Eat about twenty minutes before the meeting to stabilize your blood sugar. Or just breathe. If you're feeling sluggish, try the simple act of taking a few very deep breaths. Deep-breathing helps oxygenate your blood, which in turn improves brain function. This is one of the simplest, quickest ways to bolster your energy during a hard day.

Continue your on-the-job training. Learn something new about your profession every week. The best way to move up the career ladder is to acquire more and more knowledge about your field. Don't wait for wisdom to come through years of experience—go chase it at seminars, books, on-the-job training, or over lunch with a colleague. If you want to succeed, you've got to be like a shark and keep moving. Do one thing a week to improve your craft.

Assess your location...

"When at an impasse, examine original intentions; when you've succeeded, make note of where you are heading."
HUANCHU DAOREN

Take responsibility...
"When the archer misses the bull's eye, he turns and seeks the cause of the error in himself."

Keep your eyes on the prize...
"Do not wish for quick results, nor look for small advantages. If you seek quick results, you will not attain the ultimate goal. If you are led astray by small advantages, you will never accomplish great things."

And persevere...
*"If another man gets there with one heave, he heaves ten
times. If another succeeds with a hundred efforts,
he makes a thousand. Proceeding in this manner,
even a fellow who is a bit stupid will find the light.
Even a weak man will find energy."*
CONFUCIUS

Mix good news with bad. If you must tell your boss that you'll be turning in that report a bit late, make sure to give him a bit of good news, too. Say you've come up with some exciting new ideas.

Think long-term. Spend at least a half hour each day working towards your long-term goals. It's easy to spend all our time trying to put out the fires of urgent deadlines, but try to spend time on long-term projects. If you hope to open your own business, spend time each day on your business plan or market research. If you have an idea for a novel, write down a few notes, or a few pages, if time allows.

Be busy. Productivity, no matter your profession, is always a key component of success. If it's slow at the office (a rarity in this age of lay-offs and heavy workloads), show initiative by instigating new projects or lending a hand to a colleague. Your boss will notice. And a busy day goes faster.

Let your boss know about problems right away. Most bosses hate it when you wait until a minor annoyance has become a major hassle. So tell your boss about any bumps in the road early on. Deal with problems as soon as possible after they come up. Problems have a way of ballooning if you let them go for any length of time. So contend with it now instead of later.

Avoid the angry letter...Don't ever write a letter, memo or e-mail when angry. There is an indefinable power to the printed word—even more than just a loud argument. A letter is permanent. It can sit on a friend's or employee's desk for weeks as a reminder. So give yourself a day to calm down before writing a note.

And avoid horizontal folk dancing with anyone above or below you. Don't mess around with anyone who can a) fire you, b) be fired by you, or c) fire or be fired by you in the future. In this age of litigation and mass firings, it's best to avoid any romantic entanglements in the workplace.

...Avoid yapping about your personal life in the office ...Have too many irons in the fire ...Be determined, but not zealous ...Wear white shirts to job interviews to instill trust...Be late on a project rather than wrong...

Spread the word. When you've lost a job or are considering leaving, tell everyone you know you're looking for work. Networking is not just an important aspect of your job search; it's the single most important factor. So don't be shy. Tell everyone you know you're searching for employment. It's how most people end up with work. Keep your resume up-to-date. You'll probably need it sooner than you think. Don't leave a job before you have something else lined up, no matter how satisfying it may be at the time.

Know what you're willing to give up. When negotiating for anything—a new car, a divorce, a raise...make it a habit to know what you're willing to forego. For example, you may be willing to take a smaller raise in exchange for a higher stock option. If you know exactly what you're willing to hand over to your opponent, you'll be much stronger in the negotiation.

Pretend to care...Be enthusiastic when you're looking for work. In a poll of executives, one of the single most important factors in picking an applicant was a sincere ebullience about the job and the company. So if you don't have any sincere enthusiasm, but want the job, then make it a habit to fake it. Try to adopt a perky, morning radiance to your eyes. Imagine, during the interview, that you've just had a swim in the ocean and feel quite good about life. The best habit of all, of course, is to seek out work for which you have genuine enthusiasm.

16

Speak Your Mind

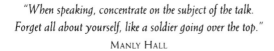

*"When speaking, concentrate on the subject of the talk.
Forget all about yourself, like a soldier going over the top."*
MANLY HALL

Read the morning paper. Make it a habit to practice public speaking over the daily news. Practice memorizing a few lines, then say them in a relaxed, informal way. Eventually, you'll find that you can memorize text quickly. Good speakers refer to their text as little as possible in order to maintain their connection with the audience.

Shake it off. A recent poll revealed that Americans are more afraid of public speaking than even

Give voice
to strong
opinions...

*"This is not a
novel to be tossed
aside lightly. It
should be thrown
with great force."*
DOROTHY PARKER

death. So you're not alone. Jangle and toss your arms and legs around before making a speech to help eliminate your jittery energy. Use your nervousness. Every athlete, comedian and spokes-model knows that stage fright comes with the job. The trick is to take that nervousness before a speech or a game and channel it into your performance. Remember that nervousness can add energy to whatever you're doing. Some performers even get worried when they're *not* nervous, because they fear their show won't be up to snuff.

Visualize a speech well-made. Before speaking, close your eyes and, in your mind's eye, watch yourself at the podium letting loose like Jesse Jackson. It will embolden you.

Conceal. Don't confess your nervousness to the assembled. It will just make them a bit nervous themselves. It may even cause them to concentrate on every little stutter and twitch on your part. It often happens that even if you're nervous, you don't appear nervous. So don't admit to it.

Hesitate...When you get up to the podium, hesitate for a moment—just long enough to let the audience wonder if you've lost it completely. And then...

Hit 'em hard...Most public speakers insist on beginning a speech with a lame anecdote or joke. This is the conventional wisdom, and it is banal. It was rare for Winston Churchill or Martin Luther King to begin their speeches with quips. Instead, try to offer up a little drama and punch, like, "We hold these truths to be self-evident..." Remember to make eye contact with various members of your audience as you speak to draw them in.

Talk to a friend. When speaking in public, try to adopt the tone and cadence of a conversation— passionate as it may be—with a friend. It helps establish a bond with the audience. So imagine that the audience is just another buddy with whom you're having a cup of coffee. This is not easy, but if you can master it, you'll be a much better speaker.

And speak with conviction...

"(Jesus) speaks with authority. When He gives orders, even the unclean spirits submit."
MARK 2.23-8

Give them facts. Limit talk of what you feel or believe. Instead, make them believe what you believe, feel what you feel, by offering evidence. Tell stories, give facts. Then you'll lead them to your thinking without hitting them over the head with your own beliefs.

Stay on the message. Reduce the topic of your speech to a line or two. That's your theme. Stick to it.

Paint pictures. The audience doesn't want to just hear a stream of words coming from your lips. They want to *see* it, as well. So paint mental images of your topic, as when Churchill labeled communist imperialism "The Iron Curtain" during a speech. The image was so powerful that it became part of the world lexicon.

Banish "errrs" and "uhmms." Avoid the bad habit of, you know, "errs," and, ahh, "uhmms" while speaking. Even if you're a rocket scientist, you'll come off as less smart than you really are. And it's, like, distracting.

Be simple...Forget words like "downsized." Say "fired." Use strong, active words like "will" instead of "is able to" and "can" instead of "might."

Be concise... As when Albert Einstein explained his Theory of Relativity to a group of reporters: "It was formerly believed that if all material things disappeared out of the universe, time and space would be left. According to the relativity theory, however, time and space would disappear together with the things." Thirty-five words. That's concise.

Be silent... Use silence to let your message sink in. Hesitate after a key sentence so that the audience has a moment to absorb the information. A good speech, like a piece of music, is often in the space between the words.

And speak clearly...

"Do not say anything incomprehensible thinking one will understand it later."
HILLEL

IV

On Being in the
Good Company of
Other People

17

Mind Your Manners

Put not another bit into your mouth
till the former be Swallowed.
Cleanse not your teeth with the Table Cloth,
Napkin, or Fork or Knife.
Spit not in the fire.
Kill no Vermin as Flees, lice, ticks &cet.
in the Sight of Others.
GEORGE WASHINGTON in *Rules of Civility*

Drink not thy milk from its container. When mouth is put to milk carton, a horde of pernicious, colonial bacteria transit into the carton. You also transfer a few drops of pre-digestive enzymes that will break down the milk's protein into a runny goop. Mom was right to scold you.

Twist the bottle. When opening champagne, it is garish to use its cork as a projectile. Instead, cradle the bottle as you would a new born babe, grab hold of the cork and slowly twist the bottle (not the cork). Your goal is not the whoosh of foam but a near-silent wisp. The more noise, the greater the release of flavor and carbonation.

Say "Yes." Forget "yep," or "uhh-huh." Show your intelligence and education by using a strong, affirmative word like "yes" instead of anything more mumbly.

Spoon away from yourself. When using a spoon, scoop away from yourself. And although some etiquette folks say it's okay to lift the bowl when there's not enough soup left to spoon up, don't do it. Just leave the rest in the bowl. Unless, of course, you're brought one of those straws that bend in the middle, in which case you should suck up the remainder. This doesn't work with chunky soups.

Slap *up*. Learn from the famous Washington socialite who, several years ago, lost her standing in the community after slapping a servant for sloppy work. If you must slap, make it a habit to slap someone who makes more money and is more prominent than yourself. In this way you won't be vilified, and may even earn a small measure of praise.

Use the handset. Answering a call on your speaker phone is a new high-tech bad habit. Avoid it by simply using your handset instead of your speaker phone, lest anyone thinks they are talking to a room full of people without their consent. And never answer your cell phone while at the dinner table. It is both ostentatious and boorish.

Remember that your lover has a name. When talking about your partner, refer to them by name rather than saying "she" or "he." It lends a dignity to your relationship to have the respect to call your partner by name.

Palm with the pinkie. When palming a playing card, use only your pinkie to put a crimp in the card. The opposite corner of the card will then be snug under the thumb. A poseur might think to curl the card using all the fingers, but the result is a less-than-natural misdirection.

Say "Sir or Madam."

When addressing a letter to an anonymous corporate entity, use "Sir or Madam" instead of the once-common "Gentlemen."

Be modest...

"When you grasp for praise, one ends up without praise. So desire not to be as shiny as jade nor as stolid as a rock . . . The person of high integrity does not boast of his integrity; for this reason, he has integrity."

LAO TSE

Lie. Prevarication is a God-given right, so embrace it, and remember that a well-placed untruth can be the epitome of proper etiquette. (Manners are, after all, the intricate dance we perform to make those around us feel comfortable.) Set some ground rules: Only lie to protect a person's privacy, another person's feelings, or your own esteem. Under no circumstances should you lie to advance yourself or to denigrate anyone else. And remember that big lies—however well-intended—are way too much work to maintain.

Lick it clean. When you've used the wrong utensil at a formal dinner, don't confess to your crime by asking for a replacement. Simply lick the utensil clean and use it again for the appropriate course. In case you're unclear about salad forks and such, just remember the simple rule: Work from the outside in and the top down. This may only confuse you more, but it usually helps.

Make sure you're not being poisoned. The age-old habit of clinking glasses together in celebration may have started a method of insuring that one wasn't getting a bit of hemlock with his rum. Participants would spill a bit of their drink into the other's glass, and vice versa, to insure that they would either be safe or all die together. So keep up the tradition of paranoia by clinking glasses.

Ignore other passengers. When in an elevator, avoid eye contact. Avoid conversation with strangers. Face forward with eyes straight ahead. Or, just for the hell of it, face the rear of a crowded elevator and hum the overture from *Evita*. This will bring a measure of excitement to your fellow travelers, which is a good habit.

Make like an old-time movie: Be silent. It is axiomatic that anyone who is rude enough to speak during films will have nothing interesting to say. Stay quiet during movies, theater and ballet performances. It's terribly annoying to hear someone yammering during a film. It takes away from the experience. If you must speak, whisper as softly as possible. If you must speak loudly, make sure that the content includes vicious gossip about a

But not too modest...

"Early in life I had to choose between honest arrogance and hypocritical humility. I chose honest arrogance."
FRANK LLOYD WRIGHT

well-known person or persons. Your fellow the-
ater-goers will be less upset by the distraction.

Give good phone. Sound cheerful and upbeat
when you answer the phone. There's nothing
worse than getting a dull, lifeless "hullllooo" at
the other end of the line. It puts one in mind of
Eeyore from *Winnie the Pooh*. If it's someone calling regarding business, it just doesn't sound good
to be anything less than bright and lively when
picking up the phone. So even if you're clinically
depressed, perk up.

Be a good tipper. The word "tip" comes from
England, where passengers would give stage
coach drivers a small amount of money "To
Insure Promptness." Most people who get tips—
including waiters, valets, doormen and cab drivers—rely upon the addition to their normal
income to make a living wage. That's not to say
you should hand out a gratuity if you're not
pleased with the service you've received. But if
everything is to your satisfaction, you should tip.
It will make the server happy, and mean good

service on your next visit. Consult an etiquette book for exactly how much to give. Or simply ask the server what he or she expects. They will usually be honest about what a standard tip should be.

Give some information. When making introductions, say something interesting or flattering about each party. For example: "Pablo, this is Ernest. Ernest is a very good writer. And Pablo has done some wonderful paintings of women with one eye." It helps the strangers feel comfortable with each other, and gives them a bit of ground on which to begin a conversation.

Remember George Bush. President Bush was a dedicated sender of kind little notes, which may help to explain how he became president. It's important to let people know how grateful you are for a gift, be it for Christmas, a birthday or a wedding. If you put it off too long, you may forget entirely. If you don't send a note, it's likely the giver will feel a bit hurt. This applies not just to gifts, but to most any act of kindness. If, for example, a friend has helped your nephew in his job search, it's good manners to thank that friend with a small note. It's an odd paradox that in this age of e-mail and fiber optics, the most intimate missive is still a small handwritten note.

... Eat crisp bacon with your fingers ... Eat limp bacon with a knife and fork ... Flatten your peas a bit with your fork so they don't roll off and embarrass you

Say "yo 'leven." When playing craps, never say "seven" at the table. Since most of the players will probably lose if a seven comes up, it is considered both bad form and luck to utter the word—sort of like saying "Macbeth" inside a theater. If you must say eleven, which sounds like seven, make like an experienced player and say "yo 'leven." If you choose to roll the dice, toss them firmly enough to bounce them off the opposite wall. If you simply roll them on the table without the bounce, the dealer has the option of negating the roll. If he does, you're marked as a neophyte. Remember, too, to pick up your dice with one hand and keep that hand in view of the dealers and players.

Walk over the hood. When a car, either foreign or domestic, has blocked your path across a pedestrian walkway, make it a habit to simply hop up onto the hood and continue your trek. If you're wearing heels or have just finished eighteen holes of golf and are still wearing those spiky shoes, all the better. The driver may appear a bit startled at first, but will realize later that you've just taught him an important lesson in civic responsibility. He'll thank you for it.

...Use your fork, not your knife, to cut up lettuce...Go to the bathroom to blow your nose when at a formal dinner party...

Make like Switzerland. When friends are breaking up, be neutral. Support both parties, but don't bad-mouth the other spouse (they may end up back together, and then you're in real trouble). Don't offer advice unless it's demanded, and even then be circumspect.

...Return borrowed cars with a full tank of gas...Take your umbrella...Refrain from frowning, squinting, and grimacing because they cause wrinkles and other unpleasantness...Avoid discussing last night's "Seinfeld," because we've already seen it...Remember that all babies are really very beautiful...

Tell people your dreams. Don't spare the slightest odd detail or Jungian interpretation. Then make it a habit to catch the listener as he or she falls into a stupor of boredom.

Do the buffet thing. Forget sit-down dinners if you have more than six or eight on your guest list. You want to spend time with your friends, not in the kitchen. And cook the day before—you'll feel less rushed and be in a more gracious state of mind when your guests arrive.

Keep toasts short. When making a toast at a family gathering or business event, make it succinct. You're not making a speech, so try to keep it under thirty seconds. And even if you usually have a mouth like a teamster, never use profanity of any kind in a toast or speech. Even if it's funny.

Have a firm handshake. It's true for both men and women that a good handshake is taken as a measure of confidence and character. Try squeezing a rubber ball at your desk to improve your grip. Don't try to crush the other person's bones. Just show a measure of firmness and strength without actually inducing pain or blood loss.

Jot notes on your business card. When handing your card to a new acquaintance, jot a note of thanks, or "good to meet you," or a mention that you should talk about the widget production problem.

Invite prominent people to your home for dinner. Don't be intimidated. The worst your boss or that famous writer can do is say no. You have everything to gain.

...Avoid discussions of work with those who don't have it...Keep your elbows off the table if there's food on it...Smile often...Remember that it is entirely appropriate to eat asparagus with your fingers...Ignore hiccups but acknowledge coughs...Pick your teeth in private...

Swear with style. If you must use profanity (as must we all on occasion), have some class. Profanity is often the last resort of the dull. So try to be original, like when Dorothy Parker, in declining an invitation during her honeymoon, responded "I'm too fucking busy. And vice-versa."

"Laugh at yourself first, before anyone else can."
ELSA MAXWELL

Point out the stuff between your teeth. If during, say, an important conference you realize that there's a bit of raddicchio on your canines, assume that everyone else at the table has seen it as well. Say something witty like, "I thought I got rid of this last week" to show the assembled your poise under pressure. Address embarrassments head-on.

Hold it right. Hold a glass of red wine by cupping the bowl in your palm. The warmth of your hand will help release the wine's bouquet. Conversely, hold a glass of white wine where the stem meets the bowl. You want the wine to stay cool. Make it a habit to avoid pink wines all together.

Remember that money is boring. Don't discuss matters of finance with anyone but close relatives and your accountant. It's a dull subject. Unless, of course, you're talking about someone *else's* money. Then go right ahead.

If you are a man and taking advantage of a public facility...avoid eye contact. Avoid conversation with strangers. Face forward with your eyes locked on the wall in front of you. Under no circumstances should you hum the theme from *Evita*.

Finish on the diagonal. When you've finished dining at either a restaurant or a friend's home, lay your utensils on a diagonal across the right side of the plate. This will indicate to the server that you've finished.

Tell one joke at a time. One *bon mot* can have your friends in stitches. Two jokes may evoke chuckles. By the time you get to your third or fourth joke, no matter how rip-roaring, people get annoyed. Tell one joke at a time and you won't be considered a bore. Don't introduce a joke by pointing out your lack of talent at comedy. Have the joke memorized from beginning to

...Avoid the use of obscure foreign phrases that no one will understand, and avoid also the people who use them ad infinitum ...When running for public office, avoid being photographed with a drink in your hand...

end, lest you trail off into a daze. Take care to smile during the telling. And don't tell jokes if you don't enjoy telling jokes.

> *"To succeed in the world it is not enough to be stupid,*
> *you must also be well-mannered."*
>
> VOLTAIRE

Be there within twenty minutes. The rules of thumb for being late vary across the country. New Yorkers, for example, find it acceptable and well-mannered to be up to a half hour late. To be safe, don't be more than twenty minutes late to gatherings.

Use a spittoon. If you must chew tobacco, use a proper spittoon (preferably made of an attractive, shiny brass) rather than an old Dixie cup to rid yourself of waste juices. Under no circumstance should the brown, toxic gob end up on either floor or sidewalk.

And remember Miss Manners. If all rules of etiquette escape you at a crucial moment, remem-

ber the advice of Judith Martin (a.k.a. Miss Manners), who has two convenient guidelines that
cover every conceivable situation. They are as
follows:

    1) Don't...
    2) And remember to...

That should just about cover it.

18

Raise Cool Kids

*"The secret of dealing successfully with a
child is not to be its parent."*
MEL LAZARUS

Let them think. Allow your kids come to their own
conclusions. Involve them in the big decisions. If
you give a child a voice in the running of the
house, she'll be much less likely to break the rules.
It will also help her develop a better sense of personal responsibility. Although it may be tempting
to be the dictator around the house, let your child
voice her opinions and make her own decisions

whenever possible. Children allowed to think for themselves will succeed more readily than kids who have only had ideas imposed upon them.

Praise every achievement. Parents should recognize and reward their child's achievements from infancy on. It will not only bolster the child's self-esteem, but may make her smarter; studies indicate that students who receive praise for, say, learning to spell a new word, seem to score higher on tests.

...Make pancakes from scratch on Sunday morning ...Play poker with your kids as soon as they're ready...

Give yourself an hour. When you arrive home, take one hour to simply be with your children. Turn off the television. Avoid chores. Don't answer the phone. Spend some time just hanging with your kids.

Eat at a table. Eat dinner with your kids in the dining room with the television shut off. One of the most important times of day for a child's development is dinner. It's sometimes hard, with busy lives, to assemble the family at an appointed hour. But it's here that a kid can talk about problems at school, hear about your work, or simply tell a funny story. It is vital that children learn the art of conversation, and there's no better place for this than at a relaxed dinner table.

Recall the past. Tell your child stories about your parents and grandparents. Children garner a sense of history by hearing about the exploits of their own relatives. It gives them a sense of pride to hear about the accomplishments of their ancestors, and offers them a sense of stability and continuity.

Knock before entering. Kids need a sense of privacy to develop autonomy. So don't assume you can just barge in. Knock as you would for an adult.

Read to your children from infancy. Studies indicate that children who are read to from an early age learn to read earlier and score higher on IQ tests. More important, it creates a special bond between child and parent and is one of the day's great pleasures. You should also try to add to your child's vocabulary by using—and then explaining—words they do not already know. You can do this from even before they start to speak right up through college and beyond.

Keep it loaded. You never know when your child will do something absurd and amazing. So have a camera loaded with film and at the ready—and use it.

Be at home for homework. Offer guidance and help, but make sure your child does the work himself. Show a sincere interest in whatever the child is studying. If you're bored with it, then your child probably will be, too.

Include the kids. Try to establish hobbies that can accommodate children (sailing, hiking, painting) and then use those hobbies as an educational tool, not as an escape from the children.

Leave books around. Children should grow up in a house where reading and writing are respected and encouraged. Leave plenty of reading material—magazines, books, newspapers—around the house to let the child know that reading is an essential part of life.

And read. If your child never sees you pick up a book, why should she? Make sure to spend part of your day showing your child that reading is not just a school chore, but one of life's great pleasures. Try playing word games such as Scrabble or crossword puzzles. Or discuss things you've read over the dinner table.

Don't interrupt. Listen to your child's side of things without interruption. If you disagree, that's fine. But let your kid get it out of his system before you contradict or correct him.

When your child is less-than-angelic . . .

Count to twenty. Or thirty. Or fifty—whatever it takes to calm down. Hug a pillow. Go in the bathroom and scream at the john. Just make sure to chill.

Take a deep breath. Say the mantra of the Angry Parent: "I am the adult. I am the adult...I am the adult..."

Imagine that you are your child. Imagine that you will be hearing the words that you're thinking of saying. This is often enough to temper your angry words with something more constructive. Write down a list of helpful words.

Display love. Make sure your children are witnesses to daily displays of affection, not just towards them, but between you and your spouse as well.

Instead of saying "bad" or "stop" or "stupid" when you're at your angriest, write down some ideas that can help your child learn from the experience. How about "better" or "smart" or "Let me teach you another way..."

Discipline in private. If your child acts up, take him away from the prying eyes of his friends or other adults before scolding him. Discipline should take place as soon after the infraction as possible, but there's no need to embarrass your child. Also, taking him into a private room helps to reinforce the fact that you mean business. Be consistent: don't give in to foolish demands to make your life simpler, nor scold the child for something that you have accepted before.

Modify their behavior. Don't wait for a bad habit (cigar smoking by your four-year-old, swearing, or tax evasion) to fester within your child. Address the problem as soon as it arises.

19

Listen to Your Friends

"If other people are going to talk, conversation becomes impossible."
JAMES MCNEIL WHISTLER

Shut up. When friends have turned to you for a sympathetic ear, let them talk without interruption. Don't try to top them with a dazzling anecdote, or even tell a story similar to their own. Listening is not a competition. If you are with someone who refuses to listen to you without interruption, just raise your hand and say calmly, "Can I finish?" Pretend, while listening, that you will later be quizzed on what your friend is saying.

Let them vent. If a buddy is sharing her anger with you, don't try to calm her down. Let her go for it. Telling a person to calm down is usually the best way to add to their stress.

...Bring soup, gingerale, videos and magazines to sick friends ...Clip articles that might be of interest, either personal or professional, to buddies...Look people in the eye when you say "I'm sorry"...

Suspend judgment. When talking with a friend, don't listen with the intent of evaluating or judging what the other person discloses. He may ask for your opinion, but until that happens you are simply there to be a sympathetic ear. You don't necessarily need to share your great insights with your friend.

Fess up...Admit when you're wrong. It may help save a friendship or a business relationship. Try a little self-effacing humor to lighten it up. Say something like, "Up until yesterday, I was one of those few humans who had never made a mistake."

And stand up. Don't let unkind words about a friend go without comment, even if it may compromise another relationship. Stand up for them. If you hear an idle bit of nasty gossip, true or untrue, about a friend, defend him. It will only make your friendship stronger. You'd want to be treated the very same way. This may not be a good habit for career advancement, but you'll feel better about yourself.

Wake them up. When a friend is staying the night, wake them up with a gentle knock at their door. Bring in a tray with coffee or tea, the morning paper, and perhaps a slice of bread and a piece of fruit. Open the curtains for them. It's a pleasant way to start the day.

Consider admirable traits. Look closely at the people you admire, or new friends. Consider those traits that you find desirable in them and try to incorporate them into your own life. Praise your friends, both for those traits and for their accomplishments.

Learn stories from older relatives. Whenever you can, get a piece of oral history from an older relative. Use a cassette or video tape. Ask about

... Choose your friends with care, because you will likely be judged by their character ... Stay in touch with old friends ...

your great-grandparents, family crises, nutty un-
cles—whatever adds a piece of information to
the family quilt.

Keep a three-to-one ratio. When dealing with
your spouse, colleagues, friends or children, it's
easy to dwell on the negative. Make it a habit to
make three positive comments for every negative
or critical comment (however well-intentioned)
you make.

Talk it over. Go out for coffee after a good movie.
There's nothing better than hashing over a
plot twist with a friend. It's stimulating to hear
another perspective on a film, even if it's just
Independence Day or *Liar Liar*.

Commit. When you suggest getting together,
make a firm date immediately. It's all too common to say, "Let's have lunch" with no real intent
to do so. So follow through. Keep your promises.
Your friends will know that they can trust you.
Making a date—and then following through—

helps friends stay friends. You, in turn, will be able to count on them if need be.

Write short notes. Instead of trying to block out an hour to write a lengthy note to a friend, it's better to write a paragraph or two. If you wait until you write a letter, you may never have the time. Or write running letters. Write a line or two in the morning, then pick it up later. Try keeping the note on the refrigerator.

Use a calligraphy pen. Write notes, however informal, with a calligraphy pen to improve the look of your writing. The pen, used by draftsmen and whoever those people are who address wedding invitations, gives the writer more control. Experiment with different thicknesses and colors to see what you like.

20

Be in Love

"You must lay down the treasures of your body."
ANGELO in Shakespeare's *Measure for Measure*

Have rituals. Walk to the corner for a frozen yogurt at 9:00 every night. Watch foreign films on Sunday afternoons. Walk the dog right after breakfast. Rituals help bolster a sense of togetherness.

Escape. Spend at least one night a week with your spouse away from your kids. It will be good for you and your partner. Go to a sleazy motel or a fancy resort. Or get three or four videos and stay at your childless home for a day or two.

Experiment. Try to do something at least once a month that you've never done before. But be safe. Avoid, for example, the use of gymnastic equipment on public thoroughfares.

Be an animal...

> "It is also fun to mimic animals like dogs, deer and goats, copying their movements and cries, to attack abruptly like the horse or arch your backs like two voluptuous cats."
>
> The KAMA SUTRA

...Light candles, because you'll both look better ...Kiss each other from head to toe ...Make love in the hall, or the garage, or under the dining table

Do your Kiegel exercises. Both men and women use the pubococcygeus muscle to control the flow of urine. A Kiegel exercise simply clenches and unclenches this muscle. For women, Kiegel exercises will strengthen the muscles of the vagina and increase sexual pleasure. Men will increase the blood flow to the penis and intensify their orgasms. Start with about twenty at a stretch, then try to work up to about seventy-five. The beauty of the Kiegel exercise is that you can do it anywhere and at anytime: during a tax audit, while asking the boss for a raise, or while writing a book about good habits. Consult your doctor or gynecologist for more information.

Make love to music...Forget Dan Fogelberg and the ilk. Try something with a bit of drama to it, like a good Tango by Astor Piazolla or a Gregorian chant. See where it takes you.

And go easy on the porno...

"My reaction to porno films is as follows: After the first ten minutes, I want to go home and screw. After the first twenty minutes, I never want to screw again as long as I live."
ERICA JONG

Keep within the boundaries when flirting. Flirting can be one of life's great pleasures, but don't make any crass statements or innuendoes that will make the other person feel uncomfortable. Regard flirting as an end in itself rather than a path to oompus-boompus. Be ambiguous rather than amorous, complimentary rather than cloying. End the flirtation with the flirtee feeling tingly, not soiled.

...Use phrases you've heard in porno films ...If you're a woman, keep a French maid's outfit at the ready. If you're a man, do the same...

Avoid your ex... It may be tempting to try to be friends, but it probably won't work. In those first few trying weeks after breaking up, refrain from any contact—including phone, e-mail, or letters, with the ex-object of your desire.

Avoid commitment to people you don't know... Take walks with blind dates. Don't get involved in a long, expensive evening with someone you may think is an evil troll. Instead, arrange to take a friendly afternoon stroll around a park. If you hit it off, take it from there. If not, you've invested a minimum of time and money.

And replace light bulbs...

> *"A man has fallen in love with a girl in a light
> so dim he would not have chose a suit by it."*
>   MAURICE CHEVALIER

When things are not going swimmingly...

Stick to the subject. If you're fighting about the dirty Tupperware in the sink, stick to the subject of unclean cookware. Don't let it spin out into an indictment of the marriage by saying things like, "You didn't wash the Tupperware because you resent me and feel superior." This is just asking for trouble. So set limits on the fight and focus on the specific problem at hand, not the sweep of your entire relationship. Things will resolve much faster.

Watch your language. Don't call your husband a lazy cur or tell your wife to "Shut up." Remember Marshall Mcluhan's dictum that the "medium is the message," and choose language that's moderate and calm. This isn't always easy, but you'll be able to argue about the issues without causing your partner pain or humiliation.

Chill out. If you find your ears turning red and your temper flaring, take a break for ten or fifteen minutes. The fight will still be there when you get back, and you'll have calmed down enough to prevent a spat from going nuclear.

Stick to what works. Couples that have been together for any length of time usually know the kind of trajectory a fight will take once launched. So work with it. Try to establish a few guidelines such as never going to bed angry, never storming out of the house, or never fighting in front of the kids. And take the fight out of the bedroom.

Go ahead and vent. If anger is inevitable, go ahead and vent before moving on to solving the problem. Allow your partner to do the same. Sometimes you just need to blow off steam.

Look for the solution. Don't try to "win" an argument, because that will probably just exacerbate the problem. Instead, look for means of coming to terms and finding a remedy. That way, both sides win.

Pick the right time. Don't discuss potentially dangerous topics just before, say, a dinner party or a night out on the town. This will just make everybody tense. Wait for a Saturday morning when neither of you is rushing off to work. Then let 'em have it.

Apologize. If you're wrong and you know it, say so. It's usually a quick and clean resolution to what could become a knock-down-drag-out.

Fight sober. Remember that a few drinks can cause some really stupid words to come out of your mouth.

Finish it. Don't wander off to work or go to sleep without a sense of resolution to an argument.

And when things are going well again...

Buy condoms from a reputable drugstore...Studies indicate that cheap-o condoms from barroom bathrooms have a tendency to break at just the wrong time. The use of a broken condom is a very, very bad habit. Remember, too, that a condom is donned before intercourse, not during; seminal fluid, sperm, and sexually transmitted diseases can all be passed from one partner to another long before orgasm. Remember to keep a good hold on the end of the condom (or have your partner do it) while removing it.

But remember that...

*"Condoms aren't completely safe. A friend of mine
was wearing one and got hit by a bus."*
BOB RUBIN

*...Dance naked
...Go Dutch on
rubbers and
diaphragms
...Stay the night
...Kiss them good-
bye in the morning
and hello at night
...Honor your
partner's successes,
but don't live through
them as if they were
your own*

Be generous...Let your partner show you their
best moves. It's likely that a new lover will have
probably been around the block a few times. So
let her take you for a test drive. You may pick up
a few pointers.

Be grateful...Compliment your spouse for something routine. If your husband does the cooking,
for example, thank him for it. It's a good way to let
your spouse know that you don't take anything for
granted. Compliment each other on your various
body parts, no matter the size or shape.

And be selective...

*"Neither shalt Thou lie with a beast to defile thyself there-
with: neither shall any woman stand before a beast to lie
down thereto: it is confusion."*
LEVITICUS 18:23

Schedule it...Put sex on the calendar, as in, "Are you free at 6:30 on Wednesday night for a roll in the hay?" It will lend a sense of anticipation to the proceedings. In this very busy world, it may simply be practical. It is possible for one to do this without benefit of a partner, but something would be lacking.

Talk dirty long distance...When on the road, make it a habit to phone home for an erotic conversation with your spouse. It will help keep your mind off attractive strangers and in the gutter with your partner where it belongs.

Think of apes...If you're a man, or a woman offering much-needed counsel to a man with whom you have become familiar, remember this habit from Ancient India: "To delay orgasm, think of a very unsteady ape moving on the branches of a tree."

And save used, worn-out t-shirts. You can rip them off your partner during sex, and then use them later to clean your windows. While having sex with your partner.

...Conceal dirty notes in your partner's wallet or purse, unless, of course, your partner is married to someone else...Feed each other guacamole in any way you deem appropriate, but go easy on the chili peppers...

> *"Sexual intercourse is kicking death
> in the ass while singing."*
> CHARLES BUKOWSKI

And make it a habit to exert great care in delicate matters...

"Never do anything to your partner with your teeth that you wouldn't do to an expensive waterproof wristwatch."
P.J. O'ROURKE
in *Modern Manners*

Be Oily. Massage your partner and be massaged by your partner on a regular basis. Use massage oil, which is not only arousing but good for the skin. Don't forget your lover's feet. Reflexologists believe that the nerves in the bottom of the feet are connected directly to the genitals, which makes foot massage one of life's most erotic experiences. As the *Kama Sutra* observes, "It is a universal rule that however bashful or angry a woman may be, she never disregards a man kneeling at her feet."

Pedal yourself into the mood. To improve your libido, or your partner's, try a bit of light exercise—a brisk walk, a short bike ride. A small amount of aerobics can flood one's system with hormones. So try raising your heartbeat for about fifteen or twenty minutes before raising your partner's.

Use your mouth...Talk during sex. Let your partner know, in very sensuous terms, exactly what you're feeling. This is especially useful during first encounters, when a soothing word can help everyone relax and enjoy.

Aim for the belly button...When searching for the mythical and illusive G-spot, the rule-of-thumb (so to speak) is that when one has entered the woman, either with fingers or the penis, try to point at her belly-button. This gives one a general sense of where this very special connection of nerves, discovered by Dr. Graffenberg, is located. Search for the G-spot at every opportunity. Remember that sex is the journey, not the destination. Which is the kind of thing men *always* say.

Practice your ABCs...Practice writing the alphabet in the air with your tongue. You may look stupid, but it will come in handy later for a variety of useful and fun-filled purposes. Do this in the privacy of your own home rather than on,

"Up until one hundred a man is still a man, if you know what I mean...But after that, it's not the same."
AN ELDERLY TURKISH GENTLEMAN, as quoted in *Life*

say, a park bench, where you might be taken for a nut case.

...Look at your lover more than you look at anyone else...Talk to her more than you talk to anyone else...And desire her more than you desire anything else in the world...

21

Save the World

*"I knew someone had to take the first step and
I made up my mind not to move."*
ROSA PARKS, on her decision
to sit in the white's only section of a bus

Buy eggs in cardboard. Avoid those that come in foam plastic. It's called polystyrene and it will remain in our environment long after our great-grandchildren are dead. When burned, it releases fifty-seven chemicals into the air. Avoid this stuff like poison, which is what it is.

Take a bus once or twice a month. Not only does it cut down on gas consumption (and smog), but it's a good way to get to know your city and its people a bit better. You'll see your hometown from a new perspective. You'll reduce engine wear and save on city parking. Even better—don't drive if you can walk.

Speak your piece. Attend local public hearings on issues in which you have a stake. Give the commissioners or council members a lucid and polite rendering of your opinion.

And throw da' bums out...

> *"In a democracy, every citizen, regardless of his interest in politics, holds office. Every one of us is in a position of responsibility, and in the final analysis, the kind of government we get depends upon how we fulfill those responsibilities."*
> JOHN F. KENNEDY

Write letters... When a congressman or senator receives a letter from a constituent, it receives attention. They figure that for every letter, there are probably a few thousand voters who feel the same way. The same holds true for letters to the editor of your local paper. There's no better way to empower yourself than with a pen and a piece of paper. But act locally. Stick to your own representatives who cherish both your opinion and your vote. Don't focus your efforts on, say, the head of a congressional committee unless he or she happens to be from your own district.

Write to writers. Compose a thoughtful, polite letter on the issues that concern you and send it to a national columnist like George Will or Anthony Lewis. You will likely receive at least a small note of thanks. You may even influence their thinking or inspire them to take on your subject in a column.

Use persuasion . . .

"When the conduct of men is designed to be influenced, persuasion, kind, unassuming persuasion, should ever be adopted. It is an old and true maxim that a 'drop of honey catches more flies than a gallon of gall.'"
ABRAHAM LINCOLN

...Bring your own bags to the grocery store to save trees, which means more oxygen heading into the atmosphere ...Turn off your computer if you're not using it for the next hour

And get to the point. Whether you're writing officials or a national columnist, make it a habit to get to the point of your letter right away. They don't have much time on their hands, so it's best to let them know your main gripe right away. Forget e-mail for sending in your brilliant letters. It's very convenient, but that very convenience tells the official that you might not be as passionate about the subject as you let on. It's best to use an old-fashioned letter for your plea.

Stay the path...Although "blazing a new trail" may have sounded good in the 1800s, it doesn't make much sense in our overcrowded national parks. Stay on the marked trail and you'll avoid damage to fragile plant life and adding to soil erosion.

Camp away from water...If you've found the only water source for miles around, remember that it will be the only source for animals as well. Make it a habit to camp far enough away to allow animals to come down for a drink.

And be nice to trout. When fishing for catch and release, don't release the fish until he's completely recovered from this traumatic experience. Support the fish in your hands, place him in the water facing upstream where he can best absorb oxygen into his gills, and after a minute or two, release the fish. *Never* toss a fish back into the water as if it were inanimate—they're exhausted and disoriented, as you would be, and could die.

Stop talking and do it. Every cab driver in the world thinks he knows more about running things than the president. The difference is that the president acted upon his beliefs. You should do the same, no matter how small the action. If you believe, for example, that the clear-cutting of old growth forests is wrong, write a letter to congress or join a boycott of the lumber companies engaged in the cutting.

...Print rough drafts on used paper to avoid wasting expensive paper for something that no one but you will see ...E-mail it to save on the use of paper...

> "Courage may be the most important of
> all virtues, because without it one cannot practice
> any other virtue with consistency."
>
> MAYA ANGELOU

Be like Thomas Jefferson. He was a scientist, agriculturist and educator. If he did not invent democracy, then he at least gave it its voice. For all his inexplicable flaws, he changed the world. It would take a dozen or so of an average person's lifetimes to accomplish what Jefferson did with his one. While we may or may not become a Renaissance human, we can certainly adopt some of Jefferson's habits:

Have clean feet...

"I ascribe this exemption partly to the habit of bathing my feet in cold water every morning for sixty years past"

(REFERRING TO HIS VIGOR AT SEVENTY-SIX).

Wear clean clothes...

"Do not fancy you must wear them till the dirt is visible to the eye. You will be the last who is sensible of this."

And question authority...

"That whenever any form of government becomes destructive of these ends, it is the right of the people to alter or to abolish it, and to institute new government..."

Eat light...

"We never repent of having eaten too little."

Go easy on animal flesh...
"I have lived temperately, eating little animal food, and that not as an ailment so much as a condiment for the vegetables, which constitute my principal diet..."

But drink plenty of wine...
"I double, however, the doctor's glass and a half of wine, and even treble it with a friend; but halve its effects by drinking the weak wines only."

Walk...
"Walking is the best possible exercise. Habituate yourself to walk very far...There is no habit you will value so much as that of walking far without fatigue..."

Keep busy...
"It is wonderful how much may be done if we are always doing..."

And make it easy on yourself...
"Take things always by their smooth handle."

Melt your credit cards...
"The maxim of buying nothing without the money in our pocket to pay for it, would make of our country one of the happiest upon earth..."

And diversify...
"The carrying on of several studies at a time is attended with advantage. Variety relieves the mind, as well as the eye, palled with too long attention to a single object."

Read before bed...
"I never go to bed without an hour, or half hour's reading of something moral whereon to ruminate in the intervals of sleep."

And grow things...
"But though an old man, I am but a young gardener."

Hang your laundry. Use a clothesline instead of a dryer whenever possible. It will save on electricity and your clothes will smell better. Also, use cold water to wash your clothes whenever possible. The clothes will last longer and you'll put less wear and tear on your water heater. Take clothes out a short time before they're dry and then iron them. You'll get a better press and save energy, as well. Remember, too, that both the dishwasher, dryer and washer should be full before every use.

Buy minimalist packaging. The more useless packaging, the more waste. So get products wrapped in recycled paper—the less the better. Or avoid packaging altogether by buying staples like beans, rice and flour in bulk.

Repair. Instead of throwing away a pair of socks, take a few minutes to darn them. Patch tires. Re-wire toasters. It uses up resources to dump items before their time because you'll have to replace them with newly-manufactured products. It wastes your money.

...Take notes on the computer screen instead of on scratch pads...Close off unused rooms...Use foot stools to keep your toes off cold floors...Flush only when you must...Buy local produce because it will be fresher and won't require the pollution of long-distance trucking to get to your table...

Stand up for what you believe in. If there's an issue you feel strongly about, then act on it. Whether it's a local zoning issue or global warming, there's something you can do in your home town. Democracy is built on the notion that we all have an equal voice in America. Use that voice, whether it be at a town council meeting, a letter to the editor or starting a neighborhood recycling program.

Brush in hot water. When you brush your teeth first thing in the morning, use the hot water faucet. The water will remain cold for at least several seconds while the water in the pipes is forced out. It's usually plenty to brush your teeth with, especially if you keep the faucet off during the brushing. You'll then have the hot water ready to go for shaving or showering without having to waste any more water. During other times of the day, turn the faucet off while you brush your teeth. You'll save two gallons each time you brush.

Fix leaky faucets. That small drip can add up to over 350 gallons a month. So take five minutes and fix a leaky faucet as soon as possible (make sure to use the correct washer to avoid further leaks).

Donate your talent...

If you can work with your hands, try building a house with "Habitat for Humanity"... If you're a computer programmer, help set up a web page for a local charitable organization. Your skills will no doubt be of great use to whatever cause you choose.

And take a quick shower instead of baths. Baths, on average, use about thirty gallons. A three-minute shower, meanwhile, uses up only nine and saves on the heating bill. If you really want to save, take a nuclear sub shower: rinse, turn off the water, soap up and shampoo, and then rinse again. It's best to try this in the warmer months.

Soak the lawn. Water the lawn very heavily once a week instead of lightly every few days. Young seedlings may need more frequent watering, but established lawns do better with heavy, less-frequent watering. Water in the early morning before the sun can steal away the water. The next best alternative is to water in the evening, but this can lead to the growth of mold and fungi. So try to water in the morning if you can.

... Wipe up spills with rags or sponges instead of paper towels... Use your own mug at work rather than using paper or Styrofoam cups... Clean lint filters before every drying... Lower the thermostat in the winter and raise it in the summer... Keep your chimney vent closed when using just the

... Keep drinks and ice water in the refrigerator so you won't have to run the tap to let water cool down... Bring a trash bag to the beach, camping, or on picnics and leave the area cleaner than before you came...

heater...Turn off the lights if you're out of the room for six minutes or more...

Maintain...If your car is making an odd noise, investigate the problem as soon as you can. Despite our most fervent wishes, it is extremely rare for an odd noise from an engine to just go away all by itself. It will almost always get worse. Instead of a $40 repair, you may end up with a $1200 overhaul. You may also be doing damage to the environment by driving a car that's burning up more fossil fuel than it should be. So have your mechanic check your car on a regular basis. If hoses or belts are worn, replace them before they fail.

Consider the fluids...Be vigilant about checking your car's water and lubricants. Mechanics believe that the single most important factor in determining the life of your car is the quality of its fluids. Dirty oil or transmission fluid can have a detrimental effect on performance and cause car parts to become rusty and wear down prematurely. So change your oil and transmission fluid regularly (about every 5000 miles for most cars, depending on age). Check all the other fluids at the same time, including coolant, power steering fluid, and battery fluids. Check your owner's manual for the proper type of fluids, and make sure to use high quality products.

And pump it up. Keep your tires fully inflated. Low tire pressure increases gas consumption and causes tires to wear out faster. So every couple of weeks, check your tire pressure and fill to the recommended "p.s.i." that's listed on the wall of your tire. Your car will handle better, it's safer and the air will stay cleaner. And it's free.

Resist the urge to top off. Stop pumping gas just before your tank is full. Topping off your tank allows toxic gas fumes to escape. On hot days, the gas from an over-full tank can expand and leak onto city streets. Your car will be fine with a gallon less in the tank. Also, once you've pumped, get the cap back on quickly to keep fumes from entering the atmosphere.

Drive away slow...There's usually no need to warm up your car before pulling out of your driveway. You'll probably be doing more harm than good by increasing emissions and wear on your engine. Just drive very slowly for a minute or two. Don't turn on the heat for a bit, which diverts warmth away from your engine.

Cruise...If your car is so equipped, use the cruise control at every opportunity. You car's electric doo-dads will do a much better job regulating speed (and thus fuel consumption) than you.

And coast. If the light's red up ahead, take your fat foot off the accelerator and coast to a stop. Over your lifetime and that of every other driver, these few drops add up to a huge amount of saved fossil fuel.

Donate your books...Unless they have special significance or value, donate your used books to a hospital, library or nursing home. You'll be decluttering and doing good at the same time.

And your blood...Local blood banks are under constant pressure to maintain a good supply of blood for emergencies. A contribution from you every few months may save a life.

Protest in peace...

> *"I think every person who believes in non-violent resistance believes somehow that the universe in some form is on the side of justice."*
> MARTIN LUTHER KING, JR.

And do good...

> *"Those who act from good motives are made happy by the thought, 'I have done good,' and are made happier by the thought that the good act will bring continuing happiness in the lives to follow."*
> BUDDHA

22

And be Neighborly

"Live for another if you wish to live for yourself."
SENECA

Wipe your feet...When visiting a neighbor, wipe your feet before entering. It shows respect.

Be out front...Wash your car, or polish your tomatoes. You have to be around to get to know folks in your neighborhood. If you do see a neighbor, don't just give a friendly wave; go over and have an actual conversation. Share a bit of news about the neighborhood, or ask how your neighbor gets rid of aphids.

And try on your neighbor's shoes...

> *"Observe other people through your own sense of self.*
> *Observe other families through your own family.*
> *Observe other towns through your own town.*
> *Observe other countries through your own country.*
> *Observe all under heaven through all under heaven."*
>
> LAO TSE

Feed a stranger's parking meter. This is both kind and a very effective way of wreaking vengeance on meter men and women. You should also note that such activity is illegal in some areas, so check your local laws to see whether you can be brought up on obstruction of justice charges for putting a dime into a parking meter.

Be kind even when people are unkind to you...

> *"It is only when a person maintains a pure and*
> *peaceful mind and continues to act with goodness when*
> *unpleasant words enter his ears, when others show ill-will*
> *toward him, or when he lacks sufficient food,*
> *clothes and shelter, that we may be good."*
>
> BUDDHA

Borrow. Borrow sugar. A book. Or flour. Or hand tools. This is how you make friends in your neighborhood. Return it with appreciation, even a friendly note if the person does not accept the borrowed item back personally.

Buy in bulk. Get together with neighbors to buy essentials like firewood, heating oil, fertilizer, and trees. Not only is it a good way to get a discount, but it also brings the neighborhood closer together. Some cleaning services also offer discounts if they clean more than one house in a neighborhood. You might also consider buying items as a group. Two or three neighbors, for example, can share a lawnmower, a magazine subscription or a typewriter.

Study religions other than your own...

"All religions can learn from each other;
the ultimate goal of all religion is to produce better
human beings. Better human beings would be
more tolerant, more compassionate, and less selfish."
THE DALAI LAMA

Drop a note... When a new neighbor moves onto the block or into the building, write a note of introduction. Even better, drop off a batch of cookies as a way of saying hello. It gets the relationship off to the right start.

But...

"Avoid churches with mass weddings or water slides."
ANONYMOUS

Offer to help... If you know of a neighbor who's leaving for an extended trip, or even for just a weekend, offer to do some watering or pick up the newspapers and mail while they're gone. They'll do the same for you someday.

Treat everybody the same...

"Treat well those who are good. Also treat well those who are not good; thus is goodness attained...Be sincere to those who are sincere. Also be sincere to those who are insincere; thus is sincerity attained."
LAO TSE

Hold neighborhood garage sales... The combined accumulation of your neighbors can make for a spectacular lawn sale. According to experts on such matters, the more stuff you have out front, the more people will stop. So get together with neighbors for a garage sale every six months or so.

Share duties…Have two neighbors watch the kids while another two do the shopping. Not only does it relieve stress and save time, but it helps build a strong sense of community.

And forgive…

> *"A wise man will make haste to forgive,*
> *because he knows the true value of time, and will not*
> *suffer it to pass away in unnecessary pain."*
> SAMUEL JOHNSON

And besides…

> *"Always forgive your enemies.*
> *Nothing annoys them so much."*
> OSCAR WILDE

Help elderly neighbors…Fix them an occasional meal, or set aside a weekend to help with the lawn or a few house repairs. Get other neighbors

And be slow to criticize…

"First take the plank out of your own eye, and then you will see clearly to take the speck out of your brother's."
Jesus according to
MATTHEW 7.4f.

to pitch in. Be like the Okinawans, who enjoy what may be the longest life span on earth. They practice a philosophy they call "yuimara" or "circle" and respect old age. Thus a 103-year-old fish monger remains a vital part of the community. So respect the elderly because if you are very, very lucky, you too will stay above ground long enough to get old.

Spread happiness...

> *"Thousands of candles can be lighted from a single candle, and the life of the candle will not be shortened. Happiness never decreases by being shared."*
>
> A CHINESE PROVERB

And call your mother once in a while.
She'd really like to hear from you.